The

DREAM
RELEASERS

DR. WAYNE CORDEIRO

Life Essentials

Honolulu, Hawaii

Life Essentials

All Scripture quotations, unless otherwise indicated, are taken from the *New American Standard Bible*, © 1960, 1962, 1963, 1968, 1971, 1972, 1973, 1975, 1977 by The Lockman Foundation. Used by permission.

Other versions used are

CEV—Contemporary English Version. Copyright © American Bible Society, 1995.

THE MESSAGE—Scripture taken from *THE MESSAGE.* Copyright © by Eugene H. Peterson, 1993, 1994, 1995 . Used by permission of NavPress Publishing Group.

NIV—Scripture taken from the *Holy Bible, New International Version®.* Copyright © 1973, 1978, 1984 by International Bible Society. Used by permission of Zondervan Publishing House. All rights reserved.

NLT—Scripture quotations marked *(NLT)* are taken from the *Holy Bible*, New Living Translation, copyright © 1996. Used by permission of Tyndale House Publishers, Inc., Wheaton, Illinois 60189. All rights reserved.

TLB—Scripture quotations marked *(TLB)* are taken from *The Living Bible*, copyright © 1971. Used by permission of Tyndale House Publishers, Inc., Wheaton, IL 60189. All rights reserved.

Cover and interior design by Robert Williams
Edited by Dawn O'Brien and Steve Halliday

Library of Congress Cataloging-in-Publication Data
Cordeiro, Wayne.
  The dream releasers / Wayne Cordeiro.
    p. cm.
  ISBN 0-8307-2807-4
 1. Dreams—Religious aspects—Christianity.   I. Title.
  BR115.D74 C67 2002
    242—dc21   2002010792

1 2 3 4 5 6 7 8 9 10 / 09 08 07 06 05 04 03 02

Praise for
DREAM RELEASERS

I believe people want to be magnificent. As we
develop relationships at home, church, work and play,
we can be used to help others release the dreams in
their hearts. In this book, Wayne Cordeiro shows us
how to come alongside others to help release their
dreams and see them soar to new heights.

KEN BLANCHARD
COAUTHOR, *THE ONE-MINUTE MANAGER* AND *WHALE DONE!*

Wayne's proven passion for people—his total
dedication to help each one discern his or her life
purpose as gloriously and fulfillingly designed by our
Creator-Father—shines through every page. Wayne
targets the equipping of each of us to do the same.

JACK W. HAYFORD
CHANCELLOR, THE KING'S COLLEGE AND SEMINARY

Wayne Cordeiro is a Dream Releaser par excellence. His life-giving message about becoming the people God has designed us to be and living our dreams as reality opens a door many of us think closed or even locked. Our potential to realize our God-given dreams and to help others to realize theirs requires only a shift in our thinking and a first step in the right direction. Any dream is possible!

JOHN C. MAXWELL
FOUNDER, THE INJOY GROUP
NEW YORK TIMES BEST-SELLING AUTHOR, *THE 21 IRREFUTABLE LAWS OF LEADERSHIP*

Release a dream and you set a dreamer free. Wayne Cordeiro was once set free from the stingy confines of a small-thinking world and has lived the rest of his life serving the obligation of his debt. In this book he has given us his geography of the human spirit. If I were a pastor, I would be afraid not to hear him out.

CALVIN MILLER
BEESON DIVINITY SCHOOL
BIRMINGHAM, ALABAMA

DEDICATION

This book is dedicated to the Dream
Releasers in my life and to the many who
will be inspired to join their elite ranks.
You will be delightfully surprised to find
that life returns far more than anything
you relinquish.

CONTENTS

ACKNOWLEDGMENTS

The gems for this message have taken me a lifetime to quarry, and still I have not plumbed that mine's expansive reach. I take comfort, however, that the treasure of its content will always overshadow my ability to capture it in words.

Let me challenge you, then, to see beyond these blurry snapshots to the wondrous beauty that lies within my focus: the Dream Releaser in *you*.

This book could not have come together without the combined efforts of many. Certain friends have stepped into my life quietly and have remained till this day. Others graced my life for only a season but left behind footprints of gold. Because of their gracious deposits, I will never be the same.

To Anna, my wife and life partner for over 28 years: You have unselfishly set aside your own aspirations and have given unreservedly to our family and to me. You are a model Dream Releaser.

To my children, Amy, Aaron and Abigail: You have followed the Lord and stayed devoted to His best. That alone has provided me with one of the greatest joys of my life. I am so proud of you, for there is "no greater joy than to hear that my children are walking in the truth" (3 John 4, *NIV*).

To Noel Campbell, who coached me out of the starting blocks: You mentored me and asked for nothing in return except that the kingdom of God might benefit. You tenderly left your gentle footprints in the sands of my soul. Each time I think of your love, my heart for people increases. I will ever be grateful for you.

To our wonderful New Hope churches throughout the globe: You are my family. Your prayers and support have given me fuel for the journey.

Thank you to my editors, Dawn O'Brien and Steve Halliday, for your tireless efforts.

And thanks to the many Dream Releasers who have encouraged and believed in me early on: Dr. Paul Risser; Dr. Roy Hicks, Jr.; Dr. Grace Flint; Dr. Jack Hayford; Larry Chapman; Duane Daggett; Greg Johnson, Bob Buford and the wonderful friends at Leadership

Network. Finally, I am so grateful to the Shimas and Iranons, who recklessly threw their hearts over the line when New Hope was but a dream.

FOREWORD

Whenever I meet a Christ follower whose life is being powerfully used by God, I wonder silently who it was many years prior who saw potential in that man or woman and urged them on to greatness. In Wayne Cordeiro's parlance, there was a "Dream Releaser" somewhere in that person's past, someone to whom the Kingdom owes an enormous debt of gratitude. *Only God fully comprehends the difference a Dream Releaser can make in the eternal scheme of things.*

My father was my first Dream Releaser. His confidence in me eventually led me to believe that my life could count for something. During my college years, a Bible professor saw potential in me that I didn't see in myself. I can still hear his words echoing in my consciousness,

30 years later: "Bill, you have what it takes to start and build a church. Step out in faith and watch what God will do!" Little did I know where those first trembling but trust-filled steps of faith would eventually lead.

Wayne Cordeiro is a dream-releasing leader. Go to his church, spend time with his people, and chat with his staff. One by one, the stories pour out about how God used Wayne to plant a seed or to water a tender shoot.

How I pray that God will use this book to lead all of us to higher levels of dream releasing!

Bill Hybels
Senior Pastor
Willow Creek Community Church

THE
ADVENTURE
AHEAD

For even the Son of Man did not come to be served,
but to serve, and to give His life as a ransom for many.

MARK 10:45

I am about to ask you to make one of the most important decisions of your life. Accepting this challenge changed my life and sent me on a heart-pounding ride filled with joys and pains, laughter and tears.

This is not a book of detailed instruction as much as it is of detailed *invitation*. This invitation was given to me, and I extend it now to you.

At first glance, the summons appears contradictory to what you have always believed. But then, God's instructions often seem to oppose common advice:

Want to receive? Give.
Want to be first? Go last.
Want to save your life? First, lose it.
Want to get even? Forgive.
Want to be great? Be the servant of all.

What you have in your hands is not just another religious book on self-actualization. It is not a motivational book on how to achieve success through applying certain sure-fire principles. It's not a guide on how to get ahead in business or how to be blessed, although God's blessings will certainly overflow as a natural by-product.

This book is about something far greater.

The Greatest Adventure of All

This book is an unabashed, unapologetic invitation to be transformed. It champions a greater-love-has-no-man-than-this kind of commitment. Throughout time, God's greatest men and women—led by Jesus Himself—all lived out this commitment.

This invitation goes out to parents, grandparents, youth leaders, elders, pastors, business people, employers, students and anyone else who wants to make a difference. This is an invitation to become a Dream Releaser.

Give your life away—when you do, you'll find it!

The Power of
a Dream Released

Part One

Chapter One

IF DREAMS
COULD FLY

*E*verybody has one. It may be lying undis-covered or as yet undetected, but everybody has one. It could be broken, undeveloped or hidden beneath the rubble of past mistakes, but . . .

Everybody has one.

It might be imprisoned by faulty character or it could be paralyzed by others' disdain. Still, everybody has one. Everybody has . . .

A dream.

All We Are Destined to Be

This dream is a hope of what we can be for God. It was divinely installed at His moment of choice. Like the crystalline keys that revealed Clark Kent's true identity as Superman, so too this God-deposited seed in each of us contains our assignment, our DNA, our potential and our ordained destiny. Hidden within lies the blueprint for becoming all that God planned for us.

His dream placed intentionally inside you is like a seed. Within that seed's protective shell is contained all the latent possibilities of producing an expansive orchard or a great forest. It holds the ability to feed a city. It can yield warmth in winter or it can produce houses for new families. But unless that potential is recognized and released, it remains richly unproductive, helplessly filled with hope and powerfully impotent.

But once discovered, it becomes a honing device, an invisible guide that navigates us through the precarious passages of life. It tethers us to our destiny long before we arrive. Granted, much is bound to take place in the interim—but this honing device locks us in on God's plan and pinpoints our destination.

> *You are never given a dream without also being given the power to make it true.*
>
> RICHARD BACH

God's GPS Device

I travel to Australia fairly regularly. The beautiful people of Down Under are a welcome oasis amidst the infinite outback and vast wastelands. The haunting tales of crocodiles, snakes and Tasmanian devils never cease to evoke curiosity in me. Maybe the unspoken purpose in my many visits is a clandestine attempt to tame this intrigue.

Of all the cities in this immense landmass, one stands out as the most cosmopolitan: Melbourne. It's a bustling city with an eclectic mix of Asians, Filipinos and Europeans, as well as a liberal seasoning of Africans, Indians and Australian Aborigines.

After one of my speaking engagements, I was treated to lunch by the host pastor. I had the privilege of riding in his new BMW, a sleek vehicle sporting all the bells and whistles. One embellishment especially caught my eye. It was a device called a GPS (global positioning system), prominently mounted into the center dash. Being a gadget freak, I was fascinated. Hawaii's cars seldom come accessorized with such nifty ornaments. (It's difficult to get lost on an island.)

The pastor punched in his destination, and *voila!* It even spoke! (Now, I don't know if my country-boy overalls were showing, but I was duly impressed!) This digital guide spoke with a woman's voice and gave us pinpoint instructions along the way.

"Turn at the next light."

"She" spoke cordially through electronic vocal cords—a pleasant tone, even if a bit eerie. I later learned that she takes her cues from a low-orbiting satellite. The navigation system detects the location of the car while simultaneously honing in on the desired destination. She then compiles the data and provides pleasant cyber directions to accomplish the current mission.

After growing accustomed to her congenial directives, the pastor and I started up a much livelier human-to-human exchange. While we were steeped in conversation, her next two instructions went unnoticed. We missed the next few turns and were promptly reproved by the unseen copilot:

"You are now moving further away from your desired destination. Please turn around!"

At this point, my friend humorously quipped that his digital assistant was beginning to bear an uncanny resemblance to his wife.

Nonetheless, we willingly made the necessary course correction (in layman's terms, "we turned around") and gratefully headed back in the right direction. If it hadn't been for the GPS, we might still be picking our path through the outback, dodging devils and wallabies.

An all-knowing God has planted a similar, albeit spiritual, GPS within us. He deposits a dream of what we can be for Him, a dream that acts as our internal honing device. God's GPS has Geiger-counter qualities that reward us with an increasing pulse the nearer we approach our destination. When we stray, it reminds us of our intended address and questions our choice of heading. Not only does it give us a true bearing, but once it locks onto its target, its intense pursuit also leaves all other motivations far behind.

This one dream, our honing device, can conquer any distraction. It defeats the most deceptive ruse along our path. It brings clarity to life and focus to an otherwise blurry picture. Nothing can rival the power of the God-ordained honing device installed in each of our hearts.

One Dream

Never underestimate the power of a single dream!

No one can deny how one dream has forever altered the landscape of America. That dream rose to prominence on the steps of the Lincoln Memorial on August 28, 1963. Under a noonday sun, Nobel Peace Prize recipient Martin Luther King, Jr., spoke to thousands, his passion ringing out to thirsty listeners standing in the national mall:

> *I say to you today, my friends, that in spite of the difficulties and frustrations of the moment, I still have a dream. . . . I have a dream that one day this nation will rise up and live out the true meaning of its creed: "We hold these truths to be self-evident: that all men are created equal." . . . I have a dream that my four children will one day live in a nation where they will not be judged by the color of their skin but by the content of their character. I have a dream today!*[1]

And that dream rang all across America. Soon 100,000 people marched in Selma, Alabama. Others picketed in

Birmingham. Opponents of the dream burned the pick-
eters' houses and thrashed their cars, but their hopes—
held in the grip of one man's soaring vision—remained
undaunted.

An entire nation shook under the power of one man's dream!

Now if one dream can do that for our nation, imagine
what a dream can do for the
Church. Think of the miracle
power available to transform
young men and women into
exemplary leaders. Imagine
what it can do for marriages,
families and communities.
Picture the possibilities that
lie within the power of a single God-given dream.

A dream can make a bicycle fly on the wings of the wind at Kitty Hawk.

When these divinely deposited seedlings of potential
germinate, the dream immediately sheds its husk and
begins to rise to its full height. A growing seedling can
split the most formidable rock or open wide a concrete
slab. It can lift an Abraham Lincoln from abject poverty
to the Oval Office. It can free a hopeless Helen Keller
from a dark, mute life sentence and transform her into a
world-renowned author and master of six languages. It
can teach a Thomas Edison to put a thin filament in a
vacuum tube and light the world. It can make a bicycle

fly on the wings of the wind at Kitty Hawk.

Solomon reminds us in Ecclesiastes 3:11(*NIV*) that "He has made everything beautiful in its time. He has also *set eternity in the hearts of men*" (emphasis added). God gave each of us an innate sense of our eternal value—our honing device, our heavenly GPS system, our dream—which, if heeded, will lead us into His plan for our existence. He planted in us a divine curiosity that draws us toward His best.

Marco Polo

I recall a summer childhood game played in the local swimming pool. "Marco!" I would yell. Immediately, frenzied players fled for deeper waters while others dog-paddled toward the corners of the battle zone. Their voices would guide my approach with the wary refrain, "Polo!" Their playful responses served as my external guide, much like an airplane's transponder signals cause blips to appear on a radar screen.

I continued to hunt my prey: "Marco!" Because the game required me to keep my eyes shut, my friends' voices provided the signals I needed to hone in on and scuttle my targets.

"Polo!"

Our effectiveness in pursuing our dream will, to a large degree, determine our success in reaching our destiny. Without the willingness to chase it to the end, we can get lost, despite having maps in hand. This dream holds the key to our development, our personality and our divine assignment. By reaching our divinely purposed destination, we can change lives, transform churches and give new zeal to old, dusty existences. That's why this dream will challenge, prod and haunt you until you surrender to its call.

In surrender you will find a victory sweeter than anything you have ever known.

> *No one can consent to creep when he feels the impulse to soar!*
>
> HELEN KELLER

Power to Transform

Imagine if all our dreams could fly! Imagine if all the potential in our churches were released. Can you picture how that would change our world?

But dreams *do* fly, and no more powerful dream exists than the one God has placed in your heart. Remember what Jesus did with 12 ragtag ruffians from Galilee? Common, everyday, unpretentious fishermen—but after three-and-a-half years, they would change the world. Jesus saw something in these upstarts that they couldn't see for themselves. Soon their divinely deposited dreams came alive and the entire world took notice.

Within the pages you are about to read lie the keys to the transformation of our families, churches and nations. So let me issue a caution: What you are about to behold will revolutionize your life. I know, because it did mine.

"Polo!"

Chapter Two

. . . .

HUMAN
JEWELRY BOXES

*But this precious treasure — this light and power that now shine
within us — is held in perishable containers, that is,
in our weak bodies. So everyone can see that our glorious power
is from God and is not our own.*

2 CORINTHIANS 4:7, *NLT*

*E*ach of us is a jewelry box, a treasure container, an earthen vessel full of hidden riches. God
did not intend for this treasure to remain buried. Jesus
reminds us: "Let your light shine before men in such a way
that they may see your good works, and glorify your Father
who is in heaven" (Matt. 5:16).

God has placed within each of us a divine treasure that
He wants to release. When those riches see the light of day,
people will see the power and the plan of God.

But first we have to adjust our eyes.

If I put a $100,000 diamond in an old, crumpled paper
bag and threw it on the pavement, most people would walk
right over it or throw it in the
trash. Why? Because we usually
judge what's on the inside by
what's on the outside. It's much
easier to see the outer condition
than the inner treasure. After all,
we live in a society that puts the
highest premium on the cosmet-
ic, rather than on the authentic. Yet the wrapping doesn't
always express the true value of the contents.

*Imagination
rules
the world.*

NAPOLEON BONAPARTE

The packaging can be wrinkled, torn or even soiled, but
its condition can't in the slightest cheapen the value of the
jewel. We can call the bag dumb or ugly, but it still doesn't

devalue the treasure within. Why? Because the value is intrinsic to the gem, regardless of what anyone may think.

Don't make the mistake of confusing the jewelry box for the jewelry!

That's precisely the mistake too many of us make. We look at what we *are*, while God looks at what we *can be*. He knows our true value because He put it there. And we release that potential only when we begin to see things His way.

Your Untapped Potential

I wonder — Do you realize what's inside you?

Each of us carries a treasure in our earthen vessel. God designed these riches to be discovered and displayed to reveal His glory, not ours. Potential includes:

- Untapped power
- Unfulfilled dreams
- Unwrapped gifts
- Undeveloped talent
- Available energy
- Unused success
- All you can become
- All you want to do

Potential is never what you have already done. Potential will always be what you can still do.

Imagine what the world would be like if each of us lived to our fullest potential. How might we impact our world?

Think of those heroes who dared to live out their deepest dreams. Here are just a few: George Washington, Mother Teresa, Isaac Newton, Alexander Graham Bell, Billy Graham.

Question: How do these great leaders continue to affect our lives today?

Answer: The United States of America, compassion for the poor, the theory of gravity, the telephone, crusade evangelism—what a different place this planet would be if each of these leaders had left their potential untapped, their theories untested and their dreams knotted within.

Still, you're thinking, *what do I have to offer? I'm just one person, and my life isn't that great.*

Would you like to know a secret? I once thought the same about my life.

Against All Odds

I grew up in the Palolo Valley on the island of Oahu. This area is to Hawaii what East L.A. is to Los Angeles. Low-income housing, wayward kids and rival gangs added to its questionable reputation and position on the lower rungs of society. Standard English had long been replaced with *pidgin*, a local dialect that fuses English with Hawaiian, Japanese and Chinese. Pidgin allows the mixed population to communicate. Such was my childhood home.

When I was seven years old, what we knew as "family" ended in an abrupt divorce. Shortly thereafter, my mother remarried, as did my father. My mother soon had two more children and my father one. I felt happy for them both, but that left the four of us "first family kids" suspended between two new families.

In order to give my mother time to adjust to her new household, my father, a sergeant in the army, suggested that we accompany him on a three-year tour in Japan. The military agreed to pay our expenses. The proposed adventure looked enticing, so we all agreed to go.

Japan provided many experiences that would shape my future. I served for some time, for example, in the local Catholic church as an altar boy. Periodically I would accompany a group from the parish in a monthly outreach to an orphanage. Even as a seventh grader, I felt gripped by the group's compassion and moved by their sincerity.

One day, I dreamed, *I will serve God just like these people*.

Three years sped by and my dream got swept under the commotion of moving back to the States—this time, not to the familiar surroundings of pidgin-speaking Palolo Valley, but to unfamiliar Oregon. A little later, when I was just two months shy of turning 14, my father loaded me on a Greyhound bus headed for Mountain View, California, where I was to enroll at Maryknoll Junior Seminary, a Catholic boarding school.

During a long layover in the San Francisco bus station, a man casually struck up a conversation with me. He volunteered to buy me breakfast. He seemed overly friendly, but I was hungry and alone, so I accepted. In my naiveté, I had no idea that his ultimate intentions had nothing to do with breakfast. Instead, he took me to his nearby apartment.

I arrived at the boarding school the following day, broken and confused. Fearing that I would be summarily expelled if anyone found out what had happened, I suppressed the memory and the pain. But for years it would leave me feeling dirty. All the odds were stacked against me.

I felt even more disheartened when I received word that my mother lay dying in faraway Hawaii. Her letters pleaded for me to return immediately to her side and reported that she had contracted a deadly form of kidney disease.

I asked my father to send me home to her, but the bitter taste of the divorce still tainted his decisions. He believed that she was lying about her condition in order to force him to underwrite my fare back to Hawaii. Once there, he feared, she would hold on to me and refuse my return. He declined.

Two days later, in the middle of an afternoon math class, I received a special-delivery telegram. As I opened and read the note, a dark chill swept through me. My mother had passed away at 10:30 that morning. I was devastated.

I dashed out of the classroom toward a grove of trees. I screamed at God, blaming Him for allowing such cruelty. I slammed my fist into the rough bark of a tree until my knuckles bled. In that tragic moment, I made two impetuous decisions: to hate my father for his selfishness and to turn my back on God for His apathy.

The next two years I became steeped in drugs. Soon I began stealing to fund my growing habit. After my second year, I could hide my illegal activities no longer and was expelled. I enrolled in a public school only to drop out the following year. Finally, I ran away from home and moved to Portland, Oregon, where I played in a hard-core rock-and-roll band.

The music, however, could not drown out the still, small dream in my heart of what I could be for God. Despite the turbulence, that dream refused to release its grip.

Dreams are tenacious and fiercely loyal!

Eventually, I finished my high school studies and received a diploma through a correspondence course and then entered a community college. There someone introduced me to Jesus Christ, and my spiritual journey began. Three months later I enrolled in Eugene Bible College.

Today I look back over three decades of fruitful ministry, grateful to God that I've had the privilege of helping to plant more than 50 churches and see thousands of lives transformed. I stand amazed at His grace—and awed at the power of a single, God-given dream.

God's dream navigated my way from the dead-end life of a pidgin-speaking waif and through seasons of uncertainty until my soul finally found rest in Him. When I reflect on all that God has accomplished, words fail me. But still the journey continues, with one bright Scripture defining my future:

> *I keep working toward that day when I will finally be* **all that Christ Jesus saved me for and wants me to be** (PHIL. 3:12, *NLT*, EMPHASIS ADDED).

I wonder—what's inside of you? Don't look at the outer wrapping or the packaging. What do you have on the inside? Don't squander a lifetime just wondering.

You have been entrusted with a magnificent destiny.
Walk with me into a moment of discovery.

Chapter Three

A DESTINY TO DISCOVER

You were there while I was being formed in utter seclusion! You saw me before I was born and scheduled each day of my life before I began to breathe. Every day was recorded in your Book!

PSALM 139:15-16, *TLB*

*O*ne of my favorite poet-theologians is Theodore Geisel. Theodore started with a dream—a dream of writing children's books. No fewer than 21 publishers rejected his work. No one wanted to take a chance on the unique, almost wacky stories and illustrations of an unknown author. Finally, a friend conceded and gave Geisel a try, publishing his work under the assumed name of Dr. Seuss. Today his classic books have sold in the millions.

Dr. Seuss has an uncanny way of making you smile. His stories encourage you and cause you to realize your unique value, bestowed at creation. I often chuckle when I read his work and wonder why more churches don't use his writings as textbooks.

Consider the following from one of my favorite Dr. Seuss creations:

Happy Birthday to You!

If you'd never been born, well then what would
    you be?
You might be a fish! Or a toad in a tree! . . .
Or worse than all that . . . Why, you might be a
    WASN'T!
A Wasn't has no fun at all. No, he doesn't.
A Wasn't just isn't. He just isn't present.

But you . . . You ARE YOU! And, now isn't
that pleasant! . . .
Today you are you! That is truer than true!
There is no one alive who is you-er than you!
Shout loud, "I am lucky to be what I am!
Thank goodness I'm not just a clam or a ham
Or a dusty old jar of sour gooseberry jam! . . .
I am what I am! That's a great thing to be!
If I say so myself, HAPPY BIRTHDAY
TO ME!"[1]

Don't you just love that poem? It reminds me how God has created each of us with a specific, eternal purpose in mind. He has destined each of us for greatness, for a brilliant future He planned out from the very beginning. If He hadn't, we never would have been born.

But He did make a plan.

So HAPPY BIRTHDAY TO ME!

Starting at the Finish

When I was 19 years old, I drove a '65 Mustang. My car, now considered a classic, appealed to the young and the restless. Back then, Lee Iacocca of the Ford Motor Company wanted to design a new style of vehicle with contemporary appeal. His designers brainstormed and conceived an automobile that quickly became a cultural phenomenon. The huge success of the Mustang propelled Ford into the leader of the car-manufacturing pack.

But it all began with a compelling and *completed* design. Only after the company had finished the blueprints did it build the machinery and the assembly line necessary to produce the cars.

Ford's engineers didn't start by randomly attaching a tire to an axle and then adding a generic piston for cosmetic balance. The Mustang didn't magically leap into existence on the assembly line en route to the dealer's showroom. It was designed and seen first in its complete form—right down to the convertible top—before the initial model ever rolled out of the factory. Long before it hit the streets, the Mustang was already destined to be an American classic.

It began in the engineer's design room with a dream, an idea, a seed.

God's Design Room

In the same way, God started on us with the end in mind. He never creates anything useless; that's just how He is. He is a God of eternal purpose and divine design. Our master designer was hard at work long before we ever heard our first rousing chorus of "Happy Birthday to You!"

We see this truth graphically illustrated in one of our most beloved prophets. Before Jeremiah took his first breath, God already had destined him in His design room to be a prophet to Israel:

> *Before I formed you in the womb I knew you, before you were born I set you apart; I appointed you as a prophet to the nations* (JER. 1:5, *NIV*).

You and I are no different. God knew what we were to become before we made our grand entrance on the delivery table. Think of it this way: He *created* us long before He *produced* us. And in the fullness of His timing, He crammed a seed full of potential into our souls and delicately placed us in our mother's womb.

The Purpose of Seeds

His works were finished from the foundation of the world.
HEBREWS 4:3

When God imagined trees, He first developed them in His design room. Then He crushed them, put them into tiny seeds and planted them in the soil. In one seed is contained all the potential to produce, not only a single magnificent redwood, but also an entire forest of redwoods.

In every fish is a school. In every bird is a flock. In every boy or girl is a man or woman who can influence many. In every life is contained all the potential through which God can accomplish great things.

Within a young, scrawny lad lived an English prime minister named Winston Churchill. Wrapped up inside a young lady awaited the noble works of Florence Nightingale. Inside a seemingly arrogant dreamer was Joseph, and within a wiry teenager named David lay hidden a giant-slayer.

Don't judge what you see too quickly! You may look in the mirror and see an incomplete contraption that you can't imagine God ever using. Regardless of what you see, remember that the master designer is not finished. You might not be able to see the classic lines of a master-piece, but the potential for greatness is there.

Since we so easily forget this crucial principle, God filled the Bible with timeless examples. When the Hebrews saw Moses as a selfish murderer, God saw the message-bearer for the books of Genesis, Exodus, Leviticus, Numbers and Deuteronomy. When others saw Peter as a rash, impulsive fisherman, God saw the rock upon which He would build His Church. When others saw a shepherd boy, God could see a king.

God is still in the business of miraculous transforma-tions. When others saw a rebellious child, God found a young Martin Luther. When everyone else saw a shoe sales-man, God had already designed the great evangelist D. L. Moody. When others only bemoaned the inequalities of women in third-world countries, God already had answered with the great missionary to India, Amy Carmichael.

A single person's ful-filled destiny can determine the eternal destination of billions of people!

God told Abraham, "I have made you a father of many nations. I will make you very fruitful; I will make nations of you, and

He hid a King in a manger, He hid life in death, and He hid victory in defeat.

kings will come from you" (Gen. 17:5-6, *NIV*). Out of Abraham's seed, God destined the birth of many peoples.

Need a little more convincing? Consider a few re-minders of how God hides His treasures in the most in-conspicuous wrappings:

- He hid the survival of Israel in a Hebrew inmate locked in an Egyptian prison — Joseph.
- He hid the great-great-grandmother of King David in a discouraged prostitute — Rahab.

...neage of the Messiah in a slingshot-
tender — David.

...ng in a manger — Jesus.

- He hid life in death and victory in defeat — Calvary.

What is God hiding in *you*?

Imagine what our communities and families would look like if we all fulfilled our God-given destinies. Just think what our churches could be like if we discovered and brought to fulfillment what God envisioned in His design room.

But why merely imagine it? Why not *become* what God designed us to be?

The Wonder of Dreams

But these things I plan won't happen right away. Slowly, steadily, surely, the time approaches when the vision will be fulfilled. If it seems slow, do not despair, for these things will surely come to pass. Just be patient! They will not be overdue a single day!

HABAKKUK 2:3, *TLB*

OK! I'm ready.

Or am I?

Dreams have a way of taking the scenic route, prompting our impatience to balloon into full-blown frustration. But part of the wonder of dreams is the timing through which God works to bring them into reality.

Careful now. I said, "The timing through which *God* works to bring them into reality." Not you! God's destiny comes only through a process of His choosing. It does not rush. It eventuates.

When James Garfield served as president of Hiram College, a hurry-up father burst into his office with an urgent request. He wanted to know if it was possible to graduate his son in three years instead of four so that he could get into the marketplace faster.

"Well, it all depends on what you want to end up with," Garfield replied. "If you want an oak, it takes seven years. But squash will take only three months."

Diamond Head, on the island of Oahu, is one of the most photographed landmarks in the world. This extinct volcanic crater stands like a proud sentry over Waikiki Beach, where millions have come to sunbathe on powdery white sand. If you are one of the ambitious, you can actually climb to the crest of Diamond Head and be treated to a spectacular view of Hawaii's most famous shoreline. The trek takes about half an hour and the final vista takes your breath away.

As you begin your hike, however, a sign leading to the summit greets each determined climber. Its words have a penetrating application:

Stay on the path. Take no shortcuts. It causes erosion.

This sign should hang in every church in the country!

Walking in the Midst of a Miracle

Don't take shortcuts. Paul reminds us in 2 Timothy 2:5, "And also if anyone competes as an athlete, he does not win the prize unless he competes *according to the rules*" (emphasis added). Shortcuts only undercut. They deface God's promise and design.

Take a moment to carefully consider the story of Peter's miracle in prison. It happened in the infant stages of the Early Church and set the scene for a powerful truth we dare not miss.

And on the very night when Herod was about to bring him forward, Peter was sleeping between two soldiers, bound with two chains; and guards in front of the door were watching over the prison. And behold, an angel of the Lord suddenly appeared, and a light shone in the cell; and he struck Peter's side and roused him, saying, "Get up quickly." And his chains fell off his hands. And the angel said to him, "Gird yourself and put on your sandals." And he did so. And he said to him, "Wrap your cloak around you and follow me." And he went out and continued to follow, and he did not know that what was being done by the angel was real, but thought he was seeing a vision. And when they had passed the first and second guard, they came to the iron gate that leads into the city, which opened for them by itself; and they went out and went along one street; and immediately the angel departed from him. And when Peter came to himself, he said, **"Now I know for sure that the Lord has sent forth His angel and rescued me from the hand of Herod"** (ACTS 12:6-11, EMPHASIS ADDED).

A noteworthy miracle had just taken place—but God didn't deliver this one in the usual way.

Some miracles happen instantaneously, in a flash. These are the most commonly known miracles: instant healings, a check arrives in the mail with the exact amount needed, prayers answered in spectacular ways, provision received from an unknown source. These kinds of miracles make the headlines and inspire the cover stories of denominational magazines.

But like the miracle of Acts 12, other miracles take their time and appear more as a process than a punctuation.

They take seasons, not seconds, to unfold. The process may take hours, months, even years.

And these miracles require your cooperation, every step along the way.

They demand our partnership and collaboration, not our neutrality or ignorance. They're like receiving a full-ride scholarship to Harvard, which stipulates that the recipient maintain a B average. Should the student squander his time and fail to keep that requirement, he forfeits the benefits. His lack of cooperation disqualifies him.

These kinds of miracles depend on our obedience.

At any time along the way during his miracle, Peter could have refused to cooperate. His weariness could have provoked him to say to the demanding angel, "You know, I'm a bit tired after all the prison proceedings. Could you please come back in the morning?"

The apostle could have declined the angelic instruction to put on his sandals. He could have taken a rain check on the escape plan heaven offered—but thank God, he didn't. With no prior clues and no immediate understanding of what was happening, Peter found himself in the middle of a miracle. Not until he exited onto the street did he realize what had just occurred.

Could it be that *you* are walking in the middle of a miracle right now? Could God be rousing you, awakening you, to something you've been missing in your slumber?

"Put on your sandals!"

Is the Lord instructing you to put into motion something about which you've been dragging your feet? Maybe He's saying, "Follow Me." Have you said yes? Don't wait! A miracle is in motion and you're right in the middle of it.

Stay on the path! Take no shortcuts! Shortcuts cause erosion, and you really don't want to miss the view.[2]

Chapter Four

DIE EMPTY!

*T*he richest spot on the face of the earth cannot be found in the diamond mines of South Africa or the Inca gold caches of Ecuador. It is not in the oil fields of Saudi Arabia nor in the uranium excavations of the Balkans. Neither is it in the mineral deposits of the Dead Sea. No, the richest plot of land on this planet is in your very own neighborhood. You might even have passed by it this morning.

It's the cemetery.

That's right! The graveyard is the wealthiest place in all of creation. Beneath those rectangular pieces of sod lie countless unsung melodies and unwritten poems. The grassy plots overflow with brilliant ideas that could have transformed entire communities, rehabilitated the lost and borne hope to the weary. Our burial grounds reek with unattained successes and unrealized dreams.

> *Die Empty! My goal is to give the graveyard nothing but a vacant carcass of a used-up life!*

Sometimes I walk through graveyards and speculate how many unfulfilled promises and untapped dreams lie dormant under my feet. I ponder the many lives that fell short of God's intended purpose.

Millions of men and women have died with their aspirations yet unleashed, their dreams now forever trapped beneath the turf. If I could mine the cemeteries in my neighborhood alone, I would be one of the richest men on the face of the earth.

The Wealth of Graveyards

Will you add to the wealth of the graveyards?

I wonder — What are you carrying inside of you right now? You contain ideas and dreams of what you can be for God — we all do. Hidden inside your heart, strapped tight to the starting blocks, is the class you are supposed to lead or the preschool you yearn to start. Locked within is the book you hope to write but hesitate for fear it will remain unread. Waiting in your dreams is the powerful ministry you are meant to pioneer but have never launched because you feel anxious about being a woman in a man's world. Those graveyards hold unpainted masterpieces and never-penned literary classics. They hold world-renowned Sunday School classes that never convened and dynamic ministries that never touched a soul.

Too many in our families and churches die rich, with dreams clutched tightly to their stilled hearts. Too many go to their graves with their potential trapped inside. If we could harness the unused power from one graveyard alone, we could change the world! But, of course, we can't. We can tap only the potential of the living.

So long as breath remains in our lungs, untapped potential lies inside us, waiting to be released. The reason we are still alive is that we are carrying something inside us that this generation needs. That's why we're not yet in heaven.

My motto in life is "Die empty!" I aim to give the graveyard nothing but a vacant carcass of a used-up life. I want the words on my tombstone to read "Empty!" Nothing left. No more gas.

Good to the Last Drop

I know of one person who died empty—Paul the apostle. "For I am already being poured out as a drink offering," he wrote, "and the time of my departure has come. I have fought the good fight, I have finished the course, I have kept the faith" (2 Tim. 4:6-7).

By the time God called Paul home, his fuel gauge had just hit empty. God was about to shake the cup because, like the coffee slogan, the apostle was good to the very last drop.

The greatest example of dying empty, of course, is the Lord Jesus Himself. On the cross He was able to shout, "It is finished!"

I want to die empty!

God has filled every one of us with a treasure that this generation desperately needs. That fortune is wrapped up inside—and the question is, Will the graveyard inherit your wealth? Will you rob this generation of your dreams? Will you deprive this generation and the next by taking the God-given treasure inside of you to the cemetery?

Die empty!

The Final Challenge

By now, you have seen the power of a single dream. By now you understand the value of potential unleashed and you realize the devastating waste of potential untapped.

But instead of rushing out to put fertilizer on your seedling too quickly, allow me to take you to another vantage point where you'll be able to see, not one plant, but the potential of *millions* of them—all waiting to blossom. Let me take you to an exciting place where you can see His design of creation from His perspective. From there, you'll be able to see forever.

Read with me these perplexing words from Mark 10:45:

For even the Son of Man did not come to be served, but to serve, and to give His life a ransom for many.

I wish I had the eloquence to describe to you the effect this verse has had on my life. Jesus never pursued a modus operandi aimed at fulfilling His own dreams. He didn't come to meet the needs of a few Galileans or even a nation of Jews. He didn't see one seed; He saw *millions* of *orchards*. He didn't see one tree, He saw His creation filled with vegetation—all awaiting a few skilled gardeners who could release the potential of His seeds and bid them blossom and grow.

Jesus came as a Dream Releaser. And that's why He summons us to follow Him, not only into salvation, but also into His image. Seeing things from His perspective will expand our hearts and our vision far beyond anything we have known.

He beckons us with His invitation: "Come, follow Me." Never has that summons sounded more urgent than it does now!

Let me invite you to follow Jesus in a way that will unleash the power of the Church, a way that comes closer to fulfilling the Father's purpose than anything I have ever seen.

Let me prove it to you. Come. Let's follow His lead.

Becoming a
Dream Releaser

Part Two

Chapter Five

SOARING FREE

*D*uring the three years I lived in Japan, God used various experiences to shape my life. The most poignant of them took place when I was in the seventh grade. This one would transform me forever.

We lived near Tokyo in a small complex called Camp Zama, an army town protected by guards and surrounded by barbed wire. On the inside, it looked like any other military compound, complete with Quonset huts and soldiers' barracks. But the outside held all the mystique of Japan.

I was intrigued by the nation's history, enchanted with the symmetry of its rice fields and the artistry of its thick thatched roofs. I came to love Japan, and I always looked forward to our weekend jaunts into the cool hills surrounding Tokyo.

One summer's afternoon, we piled into our black Rambler station wagon and headed for the countryside. We wound our way up the side of the mountains, where the beauty of the vast countryside unfolded. Periodically, a break in the greenery that lined the winding road treated us to a panoramic view of the magnificence for which Japan is so well known.

At the summit we stopped by a lookout point that afforded us a breathtaking view of neat patchwork rice paddies below. As soon as the car came to a halt, the doors

flew open and four young Cordeiros raced toward the
edge of the cliff in order to get a front-row view.

Trees blanketed the mountainside, brush-
ing the soft breezes with a fresh cedar
fragrance. We breathed in deeply, savor-
ing each moment as if it were our last.

"Ahh! Isn't this just the best," my
brother said, pointing to the checker-
board rice paddies below. Stretching
out as far as we could see lay lush green val-
leys, each one reaching toward a sleepy village.

"You can almost see forever from here!" my sister
sighed.

Unmoved by her sentimental poetry, I suggested,
"Let's eat!"

On one side of the viewpoint sat a Japanese woman
selling *bento*, box lunches containing dried fish, rice and
pickled vegetables. Opposite her stood a man dressed in
a traditional *yukatta* (or *hapi*, a short kimono coat) wear-
ing *tabi* and *getta* ("socks" and "wooden sandals") that
clicked and clacked with each step.

"Irashai-masse!" he said, tilting his voice and adding a
shrill edge to the customary vendor's call still heard around
Japan today. "Welcome! May I have your attention?"

While his voice intrigued me, it was his merchandise
that caught my attention. A large box hung suspended

from a strap around his neck. Above the box he had displayed several bamboo cages, each one containing a tiny finch.

"*Irrashai-masse!*" he repeated. "*Irrashai-masse!*"

"How much for one of those birds?" I asked, straining to understand his broken English.

"One hundred yen," he replied. "You like?"

In my junior high days, 100 yen amounted to about 36 cents. I figured that for such a deal I would oblige this peddler.

"I'll take one!" I said, handing him a 100 yen coin. In exchange, he handed me a bamboo cage containing the tiny bird. To conclude our purchase, he bowed in formal Japanese fashion. Distracted by my new acquisition, I returned a token bow and hastily headed toward my brothers.

Just then, the vendor called back to me.

"*Sumimasen!* Excuse me!" he called. "Don't forget: bring cage back when finished!"

"Bring back the cage?" I asked, confused. "I'm not planning to *eat* it. It's going to be my new pet. Without a cage, how do you expect me to get it home?"

"Oh," he replied, "you no understand. Bird not to take home. You take bird to edge and release, so can fly free!"

Without a doubt, I thought his suggestion had to be just about the dumbest thing I had ever heard. I had just paid good money for this bird—and he wanted me to let the creature go? I had no intention of complying. But his eyes remained fixed on me, silently urging my obedience. I stood there, hoping for a reprieve.

On the one hand, I thought I could make a run for it. I knew my sneaker-clad feet could outrun his gettas. But then again, there could be some hidden samurai moves under his yukatta. Or worse, he could throw one of those ninja stars at me. So at last, I figured I'd better comply.

I politely nodded and made my way toward the edge of the cliff. Before me, the ground dropped dramatically about 100 feet into the lush valley. I glanced at the vendor-turned-sentry who still kept me under his surveillance.

I slowly opened the door that separated the bird from its freedom. I tapped on the opposite side of the cage and the tiny finch hopped its way suspiciously toward the opening. Then, prodded by a final tap on the bamboo prison, it suddenly launched into flight with a jubilant fanfare of tweets and whistles. I watched as it darted over the treetops. It paused and then—almost as an afterthought—circled back toward me as if to say thank you. I watched until it disappeared into the clouds and I could see it no more.

I stood suspended in a moment of fresh discovery.

I walked slowly back toward the vendor (who no longer resembled a wary sentinel). I returned the empty cage and he bowed in the traditional form. I returned his bow but not so hastily as before. This time, I took the reverent posture of a young disciple before his *sensei*.

I didn't return home that day with a newfound pet. I brought back something much more profound.

I experienced the joy of being a Dream Releaser.

This incident has traveled with me throughout the years, forever altering my perspective about serving people. If I had even a hint back then of how much this single experience would transform my life, I would have paid 100 times as much for that little finch.

Inward-Pointing Arrows

Years later, at age 19, I turned my life over to Christ. I felt starved for attention and hungry for a better life. Yet I didn't realize that all my arrows pointed inward.

I began attending church, only to find myself rating the services as to how they affected me. I evaluated prayer meetings and even worship services by what kind of experience they gave me. If they didn't "move" me, then obviously they weren't of God.

I read all the books of self-discovery, detailing how I could achieve *my* goals and how to get *my* prayers answered. I heard all the speakers; and while each one provided some help, I still felt something missing. I had prayed all the "bless me" prayers ever printed and chanted all the affirmations taught in the seminars, but *something* still seemed lacking. The messages didn't ring quite true.

As time went on, I began to see myself becoming a person I didn't particularly like. It dawned on me that I had been using God as a vending machine. He became a means to an end—mine! I needed Him to get more blessings, more money, more position, more favors. He existed more for my purposes than I did for His. The epiphany came when I realized that I existed for His purposes, not my own.

Years later I remembered afresh the lesson God taught me on that mountaintop in Japan. But this time, it wouldn't come with a bright light or through a bearded prophet with reverb. This time it would be delivered through the simple life of a Dream Releaser.

An Early Investor

I guess that God knew His assignment for me would get taken to the cemetery if I didn't get help, so he sent Noel

Campbell, a pharmacist-turned-preacher, who invested in me early on.

Noel's wife had died of cancer, forcing him to rear five young children as a single father. I remember him graciously moving his living-room furniture to one side and removing all the breakables, so we could hold weekly youth meetings in his home. Every Saturday evening, we would commandeer his house and cram more than 100 students into his front room. The scene resembled a hostile takeover more than it did a Bible study, but you'd never know it from Noel's smile.

In 1984, I left the youth ministry and moved home to Hilo, Hawaii, to pastor the small beginnings of a church. Noel felt a nudge from the Lord to move with me — with no promise of salary and no guarantee of a position. He simply resigned his position as an assistant pastor in Eugene, Oregon, and moved to the quiet town at the base of Mauna Kea. His main assignment?

To be a Dream Releaser.

As a 31-year-old rookie, my dreams lay frozen under glaciers of fear. My immaturity, mixed with my fears, made for a volatile recipe. But Noel, in his mid- to late-50s at the time, came to Hilo to encourage and, at times, prod me until I found the confidence to fly. He made a commitment to help me stay in step with what God had planned. He remained with me for six years to ensure that

I didn't forfeit the "scholarship" God had placed inside of me.

Noel saw in me things that I couldn't see for myself. Without him, I may very well have missed the miracle God put in motion. I was both insecure and impatient — but Dream Releasers have a way of helping their charges to navigate through such obstacles.

When Noel finally saw me in full flight, he returned to the Pacific Northwest to be a grandfather to his daughter's children. When he boarded the plane, I remember feeling as if Elijah had departed! But like the mantle that the venerable prophet left behind for his young disciple, Noel left me something even greater.

He gave me an empty cage.

Through Noel's selfless love, I discovered what I needed most — not another seminar, but someone to tap on my cage. His example beckoned me to do the same for others. The same lesson I had learned a few years earlier from a bird merchant turned sensei, God was now asking me to teach.

Imagine how many restless souls are waiting for someone to take the time to bind a broken wing, to breathe in new courage, to nudge them into flight! Not until I accepted this invitation did I begin to notice the true heart of Jesus. I had unwittingly made Him into a vendor — but now I was about to make Him Lord.

Chapter Six

....

FOLLOWING THE MASTER

So if the Son sets you free, you will indeed be free.
JOHN 8:36, *NLT*

*J*esus gave His whole life to set others free, with virtually no regard for Himself. He tilted His hand and revealed His heart in John 8:36 when He spoke about His purpose. He had come, He said, to set imprisoned hopes free.

Our Lord walked the dusty streets of Jerusalem, tapping on cages. By the Pool of Bethesda, He touched a discarded life and gave flight to a broken-winged dream. On the way to Jairus's house, he restored value to a throwaway woman with a hemorrhage. And by the Sea of Galilee, rough fishermen discovered they had the potential to change the world.

Jesus was the master Dream Releaser.

The Example of Peter

The life of Simon Peter graphically illustrates Jesus' penchant for releasing dreams. Most saw Peter as impetuous, surly and a bit cantankerous. He often engaged his mouth before his mind (you might say he was ambidextrous; he could put either foot in his mouth!). His self-confident and brash demeanor effectively kept newcomers at arm's length.

But a simple servant girl easily unveiled his bravado when she interrogated him late one night about his connection to the Nazarene. As his superficial convictions gave way to the thin veneer of a shallow faith, "He began to call down curses on himself and he swore to them, 'I don't know the man!'" (Matt. 26:74, *NIV*).

Yet Jesus refused to discard Peter as a sham or see him as just another cocky fisherman. He refused to give up on His impetuous follower. The Lord knew that in this frail container lay hidden the leader of the Early Church. Dormant within this foot-swallowing braggart, the master saw the books of First and Second Peter. Inside, lost under the rubble of denials, lay the main pillar of the Book of Acts.

Jesus saw Peter, not as he was, but as what he *could* be.

Some time earlier, Jesus had painted Peter's true identity, the figure He had seen in His Father's divine design room: "And now I'm going to tell you who you are, really are. You are Peter, a rock. This is the rock on which I will put together my church, a church so expansive with energy that not even the gates of hell will be able to keep it out" (Matt. 16:18, *THE MESSAGE*).

The name Simon comes from "Simeon," which means "a hearer." But in John 1:42, Jesus changed the man's name to Cephas, or Peter, which means "a bedrock, a massive rock ledge." Jesus saw Peter, not as a spectator, but as a participant, someone with whom Jesus was about to walk closely and build upon.

How did Jesus release Peter's dreams? In what way is He our model Dream Releaser? Let's take a closer look at some of the qualities that made Jesus the master Dream Releaser.

A Dream Releaser Walks Closely

*He appointed twelve—designating them apostles— **that they might be with him.***
MARK 3:14, *NIV*, EMPHASIS ADDED

The Bible calls Jesus Immanuel, "God with us," the God who walks closely with you and me (see Matt. 1:23). He is not some cold, faraway being who evaluates us from a distance, but a nearby Lord who lovingly draws up close to walk alongside of us.

Notice the first part of the disciples' job description: *"that they might be with him."* That's what Dream Releasers do. They don't recite what you should have done. Instead, they walk with you and help you to do what you should.

Jesus illustrates this principle in Matthew 14:22-32. A mighty storm rages, turning the tranquil Sea of Galilee into an angry tempest that terrifies the disciples, who fear they will drown. When they see Jesus walking on the waves and realize He can master even an angry sea, Peter spontaneously takes a risk—and winds up in the midst of a live classroom. Jesus serves as the walk-on moderator while the turbulent waves bring a lesson on faith:

> *Then Peter got down out of the boat, walked on the water and came toward Jesus. But when he saw the wind, he was afraid and, beginning to sink, cried out, "Lord, save me!" Immediately Jesus reached out his hand and caught him. "You of little faith," he said, "why did you doubt?"* (MATTHEW 14:29-32, *NIV*).

Experience is the best teacher for lessons on faith. Without a helping hand, however, most of us would find ourselves gurgling at the bottom of a Galilean Sea. Dream Releasers turn a deadly current into a classroom and a violent storm into a potter's house. They involve us interactively in lessons of faith and help us to focus, not on the waves, but on the One who walks upon them.

An Interactive Faith Lesson

In my early days as a pioneer pastor, my son's sixth birthday coincided with a season of bare cupboards. The church was still small and my paycheck followed suit, leaving us with more month than money.

One morning as my wife, Anna, prepared to take the children to school, a creditor arrived at our home with a delinquent $200 bill, demanding immediate payment. My wife casually informed him that he would get paid when her husband got home that evening. (To this day, I haven't found out if that was an act of faith or a scheme to buy extra time, because *her husband* sure didn't have the money!)

The true legacy of a servant will not be determined by what he has done but by what others do as a result of what he has done.

She closed the front door, called Aaron and said, "We have to pray!" They got down on their knees and looked to God to provide a port in the storm.

Around lunchtime, a lady from church arrived at the back door. She handed Anna an envelope and spoke these words: "I was praying today and God said to give this to you." In the envelope she had placed a check for $200.

Now some might consider this a maudlin, well-worn story, the kind of thing that always seems to happen to others. Not this time! It happened to *us*.

Anna had the sense to share God's answer with Aaron. She drove to his school, pulled him out of class and showed him the check, the answer to his prayers. The wide-eyed young discoverer took one look and erupted, "Praise the Lord, Mom! Man! God is so good!"

Aaron is in his 20s now. After graduating from Bible college, he joined our staff and serves as a youth pastor. I am convinced that God used faith lessons such as these to unlock the potential God deposited in my son while he took shape in his mother's womb.

But it required a Dream Releaser like Anna to take him by the hand and show him the way.

Take a Moment

Why not ask God to show you a few individuals with whom you can walk closely? Write down their names and ask them to meet with you once a week. Dream Releasers walk nearby, because lessons of faith are best learned up close.

A Dream Releaser Intercedes

Simon, Simon, Satan has asked to sift you as wheat.
But I have prayed for you, *Simon, that your faith may not fail.*
And when you have turned back, strengthen your brothers.

LUKE 22:31-32, *NIV*, EMPHASIS ADDED

Jesus teaches us to pray. Throughout His life, He modeled the power of addressing heaven on behalf of others.

There is no greater support than the silent giant of intercession. Prayer opens the doorways to new discovery, shuts the mouths of lions and gives strength to the weary sojourner. God honors the intercession of a Dream Releaser because it carries the highest expression of unselfish love for another's future.

It would do us well to pause and gauge the content of our prayers. How many consumer prayers do we offer? How many of our requests focus on our own welfare and desires? If we were honest, it might bounce around the 90 percent range.

But Dream Releasers make it a habit to pray for those whose dreams lay dormant. Look with me now at a model prayer offered by another king who served his own generation as a Dream Releaser.

God greatly used a man named Solomon. The world still remembers him, not merely as one king among Israel's long list of monarchs, but as a wise ruler who drew captivated throngs to his regal palace.

Under Solomon's care, Israel enjoyed some of its most prosperous years. The kingdom stood united and Israel's borders expanded. All of these blessings can be traced back to Solomon's prayer at the beginning of his reign, a request that reveals the heart of a Dream Releaser:

> *Now, O LORD my God . . . I am only a little child and do not know how to carry out my duties. Your servant is here among the people you have chosen, a great people, too numerous to count or number. So give your servant a discerning heart to govern your people and to distinguish between right and wrong* (1 KINGS 3:7-9, *NIV*).

Solomon could have asked for anything he wanted. He could have prayed for supernatural blessings. He could have requested a guarantee of victory in all future battles. He could have made a plea for palatial mansions and lavish personal benefits.

But instead, he asked for wisdom and a discerning heart. Why? So he could better serve the people of God. He cared more for the welfare of others than he did for his own. And though he ruled as a king, he referred to himself as a "servant," someone who existed solely for the purposes of God.

This is the prayer of a Dream Releaser.

Did you know that God still answers prayers like the one Solomon offered? The king did not offer a consumer's prayer. Such prayers have become popular today because they cater to our personal wishes. But the prayers most recognized in heaven are the prayers of a Dream Releaser. Notice how thoroughly God answered Solomon's prayer:

> *The **Lord was pleased** that Solomon had asked for this. So God said to him, "Since you have asked for this and not for long life or wealth for yourself, nor have asked for the death of your enemies but for discernment in administering justice, . . . **I will give you what you have not asked for**—both riches and honor—so that in your lifetime you will have no equal among kings"* (1 KINGS 3:10-13 *NIV*, EMPHASIS ADDED).

God was so pleased with Solomon's prayer that not only did He grant the king's request, but also He added—at no charge—everything he *didn't* ask for! This kind of prayer will always receive heaven's blessing because it comes from the heart of one who serves, not from one demanding to be served.

We choose whether we will be known ultimately as *consumers* or *couriers* of God's life. What will be your legacy?

Take a moment to pray Solomon's prayer. There is no more unselfish prayer than that of a Dream Releaser.

A Dream Releaser Confronts

Jesus turned and said to Peter, "Get behind me, Satan!
You are a stumbling block to me; you do not have in mind
the things of God, but the things of men."

MATTHEW 16:23, *NIV*

Ouch! No one likes to be reprimanded, especially a reprimand like this one Peter received. But because of Jesus' deep commitment to Peter's future, He risked losing the popularity contest. Instead, He chose the slow and sometimes painful process of building wisdom.

Jesus didn't just love Peter, He loved what Peter could become!

Don't miss that truth. It will help launch the element of courage that is so necessary to a Dream Releaser. Without it, we'll be in a who-likes-me poll that produces no winners. Love focuses on the future character of another, regardless of how it may affect the present status of our personal image.

Jesus kept a vigilant watch over Peter for any deviation from God's best. Like loving sensors, the Lord could warn him immediately of demonic intrusion, rash conclusions or impending dangers that would obstruct Peter's future.

Hebrews 12:11 defines God's love in terms of His discipline, which focuses on future fruitfulness:

All discipline for the moment seems not to be joy-ful, but sorrowful; yet to those who have been **trained by it, afterwards it yields the peaceful fruit of righteousness** (EMPHASIS ADDED).

Training for Life

I had been a member at a local gym for years, but it was not until I recruited a trainer that I began to understand how to exercise correctly. I learned the proper way to lift weights, how to eat right and how to train with adequate rest inter-vals. Without a trainer, I would have spent more time looking at muscles in magazines than I did building them.

With a trainer standing over me, I couldn't cheat. No sloughing off exercises or cutting corners. I guess he had encountered several like me before, so my threats of dying and my feigning illness wouldn't persuade him. When I was ready to quit on the seventh repetition, his voice goaded me on. "Five more! You can do it. *Now* you're starting to build muscle! Push! *Now* it begins!"

I thought, *Push now? What does he think I've been doing up till now?* It was beginning to sound more like a birthing room than a weight room.

He taught me that muscle is regenerated in the final stages of the regimen. Old cells die and are replaced by the new. By stopping at seven, I would have forfeited the full benefits of the training.

Hebrews teaches us that one of life's trainers is discipline. The benefits only come when I submit to my trainer's instructions. Without a trainer, I would have dropped out at the first sign of struggle; but his prodding confrontation kept me honest—not to his goals, but to my own!

Confrontation is a loving instrument in the hands of a Dream Releaser. It is the tool of a servant, but it requires deft skill and sensitivity. Let's look at four guidelines to biblical confrontation, gleaned from Peter's life.

Four Principles of Confrontation

1. *Confrontation must be based on relationship.* If you don't have a relationship with the other person, don't even start. Without it, the confrontation will be misinterpreted. Build trust first. Peter was fully convinced of the Master's love and commitment. On the basis of that, Jesus' words could be well received.

2. *Confront the error, not the one who erred.* Jesus addressed Satan, not Peter. He first dealt

with the enemy's attempt to foil his faith. When that was done, He then dealt with Peter's mind-set and identified the drift. Never use a person's error as rationale to unleash unresolved conflicts that have accumulated.

3. *Aim for a win-win result.* Confrontation God's way should not produce a winner and a loser but two winners! It will require the right attitude, the servant's spirit, and respect for the other person's best interests. Never confront out of anger or retaliation or to prove your power. Avoid sarcasm, and always give the other person the benefit of the doubt.

4. *Assure the other person of their value.* If you cannot attribute value to the other person, postpone your confrontation. Offering any amount of confrontation will tend to wear away the other person's self-esteem. Attributing value and reinstating their self-worth must replace that which has eroded.

A person once told me, "Wayne, if you cannot express something of value about another person, then one of you is an idiot. Then the rest of your conversation will be merely a contest to see which one it is!"

Separating the sinner from the sin, however, is no easy task. It requires the skill of a surgeon, the experience of a veteran and the compassion of a mother.

A Dream Releaser has all three skills.

A Dream Releaser Protects

Simon Peter therefore having a sword, drew it, and struck the high priest's slave, and cut off his right ear.
*Then Jesus said to him, **"Put your sword back into its place; for all those who take up the sword shall perish by the sword."***

JOHN 18:10; MATTHEW 26:52, EMPHASIS ADDED

Call me Shrimp—lots of others have. I was always the shortest in my class. When I relocated to Oregon, my Asian ethnicity magnified the contrast even more. I learned to fiercely compete, just to stay even.

When the other athletes went home, I remained at the track to run more laps. Because I had learned only pidgin in Hawaii, I spent four hours on homework that took others only one. But beyond that, the motivation that began to fuel me was not the desire to *be* good but the need to *look* good. I didn't really want to learn; I just wanted to be *called* learned.

So I began to develop a coating of genuineness, rather than an authenticity that ran clear to the bone. My practice made me quick to defend my actions, thus increasing my competitive nature. Still, for the most part, my strategy worked—in high school anyway.

When I began in ministry, I packed these tainted perspectives into my suitcase and off I went. Soon I discovered that what worked for me in high school worked against me as a young pastor. Before long I was getting kicked out of basketball games, sidelined in relationships and disqualified from leadership roles. Only in my first full-time ministry position, with Youth for Christ, did my veneer begin to peel away, exposing the insecurities beneath.

And Larry Chapman was the chief peeler.

Larry, a retired logger who loved to wear flannel shirts, gently took me under his wing. He lived in a small town called Cottage Grove with his dear wife, Dorothy. Whenever I'd call him up with a new complaint, he'd invariably respond with the same suggestion: "Why don't you drive down here and we'll have some soup together?"

I guess he knew that the 30-minute trip would calm my nerves to the point where he could reason with me. By the time I arrived, he'd have a pot of soup on the stove and we'd talk for hours about resolving relationship struggles, recognizing life lessons and determining future direction. He reminded me that conflicts were a lot like rumble strips along the edge of the highway, designed to notify drivers they're veering off the asphalt. "You can curse the noise," he'd say, "or you can heed the warning."

Larry encouraged me to beef up my strengths, rather than bemoan my weaknesses. He fronted the money to buy my first sound system and encouraged me—then a young 23-year-old musician—to write songs and sing. He counseled me to choose my battles wisely, to slow down and build well.

"If it's worth doing," he'd say, "it's worth doing well." Then he'd spin some country horse-sense adages: "Sure, you're bound to make some mistakes along the way. That's only evidence that you're going somewhere. The only time you don't make mistakes is if you're standing still." Then he'd scratch his head, smile and say, almost as an afterthought, "But then again, if you're going too fast, you can't take the turns, neither. Slow down and watch the signs. God put 'em there for a reason."

Larry was a Dream Releaser. He knew how to protect me from my own unharnessed ambitions. He taught me how to sheath my sword and cool my jets. He taught me to read the signs, instead of cursing them.

Larry's gone now, but he left behind his impression on my soul. My life would be vastly different today if he had not walked into it for a brief season. I look forward to seeing him in heaven one day. And I suspect that as soon as we meet, he'll say, "Come on in. Let's have some soup together."

The Invitation

Imagine what the twenty-first century Church could look like if God's children were *living* their dreams. We need to raise up a new generation of men and women who not only realize the power of dreams but also understand that those dreams will remain untapped unless we commit to becoming Dream Releasers.

Help others achieve their dreams, and you will achieve yours.

LES BROWN

You might ask, "But what about my own dreams? What will become of them?"

The answer to that question is given only to those who believe in promises. When anyone chooses to relinquish his own life for that of another's, all of heaven takes notice. For these the master Dream Releaser personally steps in and gladly takes the honor to fulfill the undeveloped dreams.

To Him we could pay no higher tribute!

For whoever wants to save his life will lose it, but whoever loses his life for me will find it.

MATTHEW 16:25, *NIV*

Chapter Seven

DREAM KILLERS

I had a dream my life would be . . .
So different now from what it seemed.
Now life has killed the dream I dreamed.

"I Dreamed a Dream," *Les Miserables*

*O*ver the years I have closely watched several world-class tennis players, as well as many Olympic figure skaters. In nearly every case, I have seen a common practice: they always travel with a coach.

A *coach*? These young men and women are some of the best around! Why in the world would they need a coach?

Answer: That's why they *are* the best in the world. They understand the importance of a coach. Coaches can make the difference between winning and losing.

A Dream Releaser is a kind of coach. Like tour guides, Dream Releasers lead us through the jungles of important decisions. They will hunt down the tigers that "tear your hope apart as they turn your dreams to shame."[1]

Often, the greatest ideas, the most monumental thoughts and the most creative answers lay suffocating beneath the rubble of mistakes, character flaws, the fear of failure, a history of rejection, the fear of accountability or personality quirks. These are dream killers.

Dream killers don't line up like redcoats in battle. Like guerilla fighters, they stalk you until they surround you. They challenge you from without and taunt you from within.

A dream killer can take many forms. It could appear as pride or fear. It could show up as anger or passivity.

It could take the form of greed or come wrapped in the burlap of unworthiness. Whatever form it takes, this murderer robs us of our future and siphons off our potential.

Our families, churches and relationships desperately need dream-releasing coaches to help us identify and defeat these killers of potential. Without such coaches, the tigers will prey on us until they consume our futures, one dream at a time.

One of the Dream Releaser's greatest roles is a coach of character, not a judge of it. We all have a surplus of people eager to judge us, but what we desperately require are coaches who will offer guidance. We all search for friends who will safely steer us through life's maze of deliberations and decisions.

From a coach's perspective, let's take a look at eight dream killers. At the end of each section you will be invited to participate in a Take a Moment exercise that will help to catalyze the lesson and etch each new perspective deeper into your heart.

Dream Killer #1: Unproven Character

*We also exult in our tribulations, knowing that tribulation brings about perseverance; and perseverance, proven character; and **proven character**, hope.*

ROMANS 5:3-4, EMPHASIS ADDED

The major difference between novices and veterans is that the former have hundreds of mistakes inside of them just waiting to be made. These mistakes will either dissolve with coaching or they will become land mines waiting to be detonated by the heavy footfall of a character deficiency.

Someone once said, "You will be ruled by the rudder or you will be ruled by the rocks." Character is like a rudder; without it we will end up on the rocks. We need that rudder, especially when life's inevitable storms hit.

I don't like storms, but I have to admit that I like what they can produce. I don't like running, but I like the health and conditioning that it produces. I don't like disciplining myself; but that discipline produces clarity of mind, a clear conscience, and a thousand more benefits. I don't like to stop for gasoline, but without it my car sits motionless, so I take the time to pop the gas cover and fill the tank.

Storms fall into the same category. We may not like them, but when we correctly handle them, they bring about benefits unobtainable in any other setting.

As a coach, you must remind your young dreamers that the first step in surviving any storm is to outlast it. It is *perseverance* that brings about proven character. Help them to meet storms head-on, with a heart that refuses to give up, not out of stubbornness, but from a commitment to God's best. Quelling any desire to surrender will turn *potential* character into *proven* character. Isaiah 48:10 declares that God is refining us and testing us in the furnace of affliction. Only in the fire does God's alchemy turn "potential" into "proven."

God has hardwired into your charges the image of His Son, Jesus Christ—not 10 percent of His image, not 70 percent, but 100 percent. He plans for them to attain to the fullness of His image, and He made His plan 100 percent achievable. That image, however, is in seed form. And His favorite tool to pry it out?

Pain.

When I Was Your Age

But the Lord said to him, "Go, for he is a chosen instrument of Mine, to bear My name before the Gentiles and kings and the sons of Israel; for I will show him how much he must suffer for My name's sake."
ACTS 9:15-16, EMPHASIS ADDED

During my son Aaron's high school years, the two of us met for devotions three times a week before school. I still count those meetings among our best times together as father and son. We would meet at a local coffee shop and read a few chapters from the Bible. Then after recording our observations in our respective journals, we'd spend a few minutes sharing the treasures we had mined.

Even though Aaron has since graduated from Bible college, we continue the practice today. One day, as college graduation drew near, he proudly said, "Well, Dad, soon I will have my degree in theology and I will be ready for ministry!"

"Not yet," I said with a laugh.

"What do you mean? I've completed all my classes. What's left?"

"You haven't yet suffered enough."

Then I pointed out that when *I* was his age, I had to walk two miles to and from college, both ways uphill. I paid my own tuition, darned my own socks and grew my own food.

Then we both laughed.

At the risk of turning the jovial into the macabre, I reminded my son that I was indeed serious. Certain character qualities will be refined only in the crucible of suffering. Who has the greatest compassion for those who have been abused or molested or have suffered through some terrible disease? Someone who has been there.

Suffering will change a young dreamer—but not necessarily for the better. God wants you to help your young dreamer choose to use pain redemptively. Handled poorly, suffering will make a person angry. Encourage your dreamers to remember this: Anger is like a homemade bomb strapped around one's waist. Whoever detonates the bomb becomes a suicide bomber. They not only injure anyone in the near vicinity, but *they* go up as well. Anger destroys their reputation, devastates friendships and, worst of all, amputates their potential.

> *There are two pains in life: the pain of discipline and the pain of regret.*

Take a Moment

Encourage your dreamers to pray this prayer designed to help them position their hearts to receive His work:

> Heavenly Father, how I want to look like You in every respect—in heart, thought, spirit and action. I have only one lifetime to give to You. This is my only opportunity, so refine me until **potential** character becomes **proven** character. I give You permission to test my faith as You see fit.
>
> I know this is a dangerous prayer. My flesh is screaming at me to stop and recant—but I must not. I love You too much and I love

what You can make of me. You bore the Cross
for me! That puts it all into perspective. Amen.

Dream Killer #2: Pride

Do you want to know one of the fastest ways to kill your
potential? Become overly impressed with your accomplishments. Awards may pleasantly affirm performance,
but they remain empty of potential.

Though we never met face-to-face, I consider Mother
Teresa one of my dearest mentors. She changed the world
(and received the coveted Nobel Peace Prize) by unselfishly bringing God's love to the poorest of the poor in
Calcutta. In one of her books she recorded several of her
prayers. One in particular struck my heart. Every morning, she began her day by saying this: "Lord, may I truly
begin serving You, starting today; for up to now, I have
really done nothing."

Nothing? Mother Teresa accomplished far more than
I can even imagine. Over time I came to understand that she
didn't mean to demean her efforts but to express her heart.
She refused to be satisfied with what her order already
had accomplished. She kept her eyes on what could yet be
done and refused to feel satisfied with accolades.

Her attitude reminds me of the apostle Paul's, who
wrote, "I do not regard myself as having laid hold of it

yet; but one thing I do: forgetting what lies behind and reaching forward to what lies ahead, I press on toward the goal for the prize of the upward call of God in Christ Jesus" (Phil. 3:13-14).

Don't permit your dreamers to build an altar to their accomplishments. Dissuade them from spending too much time polishing their trophies. Discourage them from burning incense to their successes. Rather, show them how to thank God for His goodness and press on to what lies ahead.

How can you best keep pride at bay? Never let yourself or your dreamers forget that we are all servants. It doesn't matter how many thousands we may address during the day or how many interviews we give on the evening news. When night falls, we return to the servant's quarters. No one sleeps in the palace but the King!

What should happen if, on the following day, the master asks us to clean urinals? How will we answer? Jesus wants us to respond with the same exuberance as when He asked us to speak to thousands. He commissions us every day, and His assignment can change without notice. Ask Saul. Ask Eli. Ask Judas.

Ask Rehoboam.

Misplaced Confidence

It took place when the kingdom of Rehoboam was established and strong that he and all Israel with him forsook the law of the LORD.

2 CHRONICLES 12:1

Pride often results from poorly stewarded confidence. How quickly we can mistake a measure of success for invincibility! That's exactly what happened to Rehoboam, who duped himself into thinking he was indestructible. The fiercest of exams interrogated him: success.

Remember, the greatest test of faith is not poverty. Poverty might refine you, but it's *prosperity* that will ruthlessly examine you.

While confidence can coexist with humility, pride cannot. Confidence remains teachable; pride refuses to learn. Confidence expresses itself in gratitude; pride demands accolades. Confidence draws people to you; pride repels them.

Before he was Mohammed Ali, he was Cassius Clay. The name changed, but his brash, cocky demeanor remained. On a commercial flight to a boxing match, a flight attendant instructed him to fasten his seat belt for takeoff.

"I'm Superman," he boasted. "Superman don't need no seatbelt!"

When the flight attendant politely repeated her request, Ali curtly replied, "I said I'm Superman, and Superman don't need no seat belt."

Unflustered, the woman confidently answered, "Superman don't need no airplane either. Now put on your seat belt!"

He complied.

Take a Moment

Plan a time when you can get together with your group of dreamers. Talk about the differences between confidence and pride. Identify the telltale markings of pride's subtle disguises. Point out the dangers ahead and coach them through the uncertain terrain that accompanies success.

Dream Killer #3: Impatience

Learn to be patient, so that you will please God and be given what he has promised.
HEBREWS 10:36, *CEV*

Impatience kills dreamers like heart disease kills Americans. It can be detected through the symptoms of unwise decisions, inappropriate timing, financial irresponsibility or an aversion to gaining permission.

We've seen it in the best. Abraham's impatience resulted in Ishmael, whose arrival caused a broken relationship and two nations that continue to feud to this day.

Impatience compromises our ability to wait until God determines we are ready. We try to occupy the penthouse while He's still building the foundation. Impatience causes us to forget that positions come with responsibilities, houses need maintenance, relationships demand accountability, love comes at a large cost and leadership brings problems. We want the glitter but not the litter, the gain but not the pain, the prize without the investment.

Young dreamers are often impetuous and quick on the draw. They resemble amateur pianists who choose speed over accuracy, trying in their haste to play arpeggios faster than their ability allows. Unless a coach intervenes and challenges this tendency, a young dreamer may trade clarity for the impression of swiftness—and their aversion to practicing scales will rob them of the strengths needed to take them to the finish.

Training in the Harness

For my junior and senior years of high school I attended a small country school where I ran track. I did the sprints, triple jump, pole vault and relay. We practiced on a cinder track and ran through nearby pastures for training. (The coach claimed that it would build lateral strength from dodging the cow pies that lay scattered like land mines.)

Our coach also used a sprinter's harness—basically a vest attached to a telephone pole by ropes and pulleys—to assist in our training. The coach could regulate the speed of a sprinter using this antiquated contraption.

I remember strapping on the vest and Coach reeling me into the blocks. At the firing of a starting pistol, I pushed out of my starting position, cinders spraying like shrapnel from my track cleats. Coach slowly let out more rope, prolonging my tug-of-war with the telephone pole. I felt like a hooked marlin trying to escape a determined fisherman.

With time and patience the mulberry leaf becomes a silk gown.
CHINESE PROVERB

But in this slow-motion pose, the coach could adjust my form and correct my running posture. Best of all, the device built the "quick twitch muscles" required for sprinters. After 30 seconds or so, the coach would blow his whistle to end the ordeal. He'd reel me in and we'd start the whole chase over again.

Coach would continually remind me, "This exercise will build the correct muscles and tensile strength you'll need for endurance. You will have the adequate stamina and power to take you to the finish line without your speed decreasing in the last few yards."

I always looked forward to the final sprint of the day — the one without the vest. When Coach fired the starter's pistol, I came out of the blocks like a rocket.

Staying in the Harness

Come to Me, all who are weary and heavy-laden,
and I will give you rest. Take My yoke upon you, and learn
from Me, for I am gentle and humble in heart; and
you shall find rest for your souls.

MATTHEW 11:28-29

Everyone starts with only a promise — and a harness.

The promise of your dreamers' future will always remain greater than their present ability. God will always give them dreams that are further along than their current level of maturity. That means that their present ability will not take them the distance. With that in mind, God locks them in on their destiny, fits them into His harness and begins the training process.

God did this with Joseph. At the time the Lord gave Joseph a remarkable dream, Joseph's character lacked the tensile strength built only on the cinder track of experience. Many years and many lessons were yet to come. His regimen included a long walk in the hot desert, slavery, false accusation and a stint in prison. His route took him through a vale of sorrow, a wrestling match with anger and the temptation to use his power to quench his thirst for revenge. His training wounded him and then healed him. He received his education in the prison of despair, and the villain of temptation interrogated him.

But he stayed in the harness.

God did the same thing with David. In 1 Samuel 16, the prophet anoints David the king of Israel—but it would be 18 long chapters before he'd actually take the throne. His training required courses in everything from ducking spears to a seven-year manhunt. He became as adept at hiding in caves as he was at hiding his pain in the lines of poetic rhyme. He was stalked, loved and despised. He even bore the stinging guilt of a tardy arrival, which could have saved his own city from destruction.

But he stayed in the harness.

God did the same thing with Mary. The Lord chose her among all women of all time to bear the Messiah. Yet this young teenaged girl had no idea of the trials she'd face. Townspeople slandered her and gossiped about her. Her fiancé, suspecting infidelity, nearly broke their engagement. Family members shunned her; friends abandoned her. Eventually circumstances forced her to flee to Egypt.

The way to succeed is never quit. That's it.

ALEX HALEY

But she stayed in the harness.

And God does the same thing with each of us. If your dreamers are to see their dreams take flight, they must develop the critical character qualities of endurance, integrity, wisdom, discernment, selflessness, stewardship and authenticity—none of which appear overnight. They come only to those who stay in the harness.

I love what Calvin Coolidge once said:

> *Nothing in this world can take the place of persistence. Talent will not; nothing is more common than unsuccessful people with talent. Genius will not; unrewarded genius is almost a proverb. Education will not; the world is full of educated derelicts. Persistence and determination alone are omnipotent. The slogan "press on" has solved and always will solve the problems of the human race.*[2]

Every young dreamer must overcome impatience. A seasoned coach can help him or her to develop the discipline and self-control that success requires. So, Coach, encourage your young dreamers to stay in the harness. Remind them that they have no choice if they plan to go the distance.

Take a Moment
Consider the character qualities that God wants to build in your young dreamers. What disciplines make up the loving harness that God has placed on them? Help them to remember that He says, "Take My yoke upon you." His harness fits perfectly!

Dream Killer #4: Ingratitude

In everything give thanks; for this is God's will for you in Christ Jesus.
1 THESSALONIANS 5:18

God feels more concerned about our thankfulness than He does about almost anything else. A grateful child gains his parents' delight. An ungrateful child gains only their disappointment.

Nothing isolates you from others more quickly than ungratefulness!

One hot afternoon, the disciples faced a hungry mob of 4,000 men, plus women and children. Jesus used the volatile occasion to teach his young Dream Releasers a tremendous lesson about thankfulness. "Where could we get enough bread in this remote place to feed such a crowd?" the disciples asked their master (Matt 15:32).

> *"How many loaves do you have?" Jesus asked. "Seven," they replied, "and a few small fish." He took the seven loaves and the fish, and **when he had given thanks,** he broke them and gave them to the disciples* (MATT. 15:34, 36, *NIV,* EMPHASIS ADDED).

Jesus didn't grumble over the apparent lack. He didn't lobby for more. Instead, He gave thanks for what He had and started to minister with that. Teach your young dreamers to give thanks for what they have. Don't let them wait for a guarantee. Often, the impossible is simply the untried. Show them how to be grateful and launch out with what they have.

Please the Father

When Aaron was five years old, we moved into a new neighborhood. He took his bicycle and, like any other active boy, set out on a search for new friends. He returned a little while later with a new buddy in tow. As they chugged up the driveway, I noticed a loose chain on his friend's bike, dragging on the asphalt.

"Hey, Dad," Aaron said, "this is my friend Jamie. His bike broke and it won't pedal anymore. You think it could be fixed?"

A brief investigation revealed that a chain had slipped off the bike's sprocket. A screwdriver and half a turn of the sprocket would quickly remedy the problem. But here I had an opportunity to combine two naïve kids with a mischievous dad. I wrinkled my brow, scratched my chin and said, "Hmm. I dunno, Aaron. It looks pretty gnarly to me."

"But, Dad, he's my friend. Couldn't you try to fix it?"

"W-e-l-l," I said slowly, milking the word for all it was worth. Then I began to spin my playful diagnosis.

"It looks like the medial protractor has slipped from the internal core fibulator. And that instigated a gyrofractic reaction, causing the chain to ruminate excessively. It doesn't look too promising." I furrowed my brow, shook my head and then declared, "But since it's for you, Aaron, Dad's going to go for it!"

> *We need to be more grateful. There is no true character without gratitude. To have feelings of gratitude is one of the marks of a strong character. We need more of that spirit in our homes and our daily associations.*
>
> EZRA TAFT BENSON

With renewed excitement, Aaron turned to his new friend. "Watch this!" he said proudly. "My dad can fix *anything*!"

When I heard his five-year-old heart of gratefulness, I not only got ready to fix the slipped chain, but I also determined to paint the whole bike and buy him new tires to boot!

Our heavenly Father responds in much the same way to His own grateful children. For them, He will open up the windows of heaven and pour out His blessings. Whenever God sees a grateful heart, He feels great delight. Make sure your young dreamers understand the key place of gratitude.

Make Me More Like You!

How do you coach gratefulness? You start by modeling it. Gratitude cannot be defined into existence, only "exampled." It starts with us. How often I have observed a genuine expression of gratitude and found myself silently praying, "Oh, God, please develop that in me too!"

A spirit of gratefulness is more than a dutiful "Thank you." Gratitude takes the time to express fully the positive impact of another person's life or actions. Those who feel truly grateful invest the time to speak in detail how they are different today because of what others have done.

It takes practice to properly express gratitude. Our fallen humanity wars against such humility, but humility produces the most genuine hearts.

Take a Moment

Write down the names of three people who have invested in you. Devote a few minutes to each one, pondering how you might genuinely communicate your gratitude. It might be in the form of a note, a gift or a meal or in verbal form. But let each expression enumerate *why* the individual means so much to you. By making this a practice, over time you will instinctively begin to model gratefulness for your young dreamers.

Dream Killer #5: Incorrectability

The rod and reproof give wisdom, but a child who gets his own way brings shame.

PROVERBS 29:15

Suffering comes in many forms, and none of them fall under the category of fun. Suffering always changes us but not necessarily for the better; *we* must choose that. Pain will test everything about us, but the most telling thing it reveals is our "correctability factor."

How correctable are you and your young dreamers? Correctability is one of the most important factors in the growth process. Its presence or absence in your life will determine your fruitfulness, the quality and health of your relationships and your resilience. It is your spiritual IQ. It reveals your ability to respond quickly to the truth that God reveals to you.

Shortly after His resurrection, Jesus gauged the correctability factor of two confused sojourners. Their inadequate understanding of the past week's events caught them unprepared for the flood of doubts that crowded their hearts. "We were hoping that it was He who was going to redeem Israel!" they complained (Luke 24:21), not realizing that the One who walked with them was the very One who had died and risen again.

Jesus patiently explained to them the Scriptures, proving from the prophets that the Cross had to occur. Their barbed questions revealed their skepticism, however, and they remained unconvinced. So Jesus said to them,

"O *foolish* men and *slow of heart* to believe in all that the prophets have spoken!" (Luke 24:25, emphasis added).

Does calling someone "foolish" and "slow of heart" sound like a kind way to address an individual? It really is, if that's what it takes to dislodge the person from serious error so that he or she can spiritually move forward once again.

Inside each of our hearts is a "Correctability Meter" that comes with a calibration knob featuring three settings: slow, medium and fast. The two disciples on the road to Emmaus had set their meters on slow, which caused their hearts to dim.

How can you increase your correctability factor? How can you increase that of your young dreamers?

Proverbs introduces us to two of life's instructors: Wisdom and Consequences. Both are excellent teachers, and both exact a price.

Wisdom beckons us in the very first chapter: "Turn to my reproof, behold, I will pour out my spirit on you; I will make my words known to you" (Prov. 1:23). Wisdom makes herself available on a "first come, first served" basis. Notice the salient phrase: "first come"! Wisdom doesn't chase after anyone. Instead, she instructs us to "turn to" her. We need to enroll in her course and come to her school. She puts the ball of learning into our court.

Should we choose not to enroll, by default we will land in the classroom of the second great teacher, Consequences. This instructor will come to you, but his price is steep. By the time you graduate from his course, you may have lost years, your ministry, your marriage and even your family.

Each of us has two windows of opportunity to correct a mistake. Wisdom will teach us how to correct the error before we commit it. Consequences will require us to commit the act first and then choose whether we will correct it later.

Choose Wisdom! It hurts a lot less.

To avail yourself of Wisdom, however, you must turn to her reproof and correction. I have watched many potential-filled individuals disqualify themselves by retreating from an opportunity to be evaluated. In refusing to increase their correctability factor, their endurance flagged and their faith grew anemic. Unwilling to suffer for the sake of growth, they

You will choose between two teachers in life: Wisdom or Consequences.

forfeited another hallmark of every great leader — correctability. Teach your dreamers to remain open to correction and to maintain that attitude until the Lord takes them home.

Take a Moment

Scan the book of Proverbs and identify the instructions of Wisdom. Make a list of her directives and commit them to your soul. They will teach you and instruct you (and your dreamers!) in the way that you should go. She will be an ever-present voice to counsel you as you develop the heart of a Dream Releaser.

Dream Killer #6: Unbelief

I am not ashamed; for I know whom I have believed
and I am convinced that He is able.

2 TIMOTHY 1:12

Unbelief sends more potential and dreams to the grave than we will ever know.

We often give events and challenges in our lives a "measure of difficulty" rating, much like judges in a gymnastics contest. Such a practice dictates, to a large extent, the level of faith we muster in order to accomplish a task. If the assignment seems too difficult, our excuses abound and the reasons for our underachievement begin. Too often we settle for one of the consolation brackets with one of three sorry laments: "Could've," "Should've" or "Would've."

Nothing could be further from God's design. The apostle Paul reminds us to "run in such a way that you may win" (1 Cor. 9:24). When it comes to releasing the potential of your young dreamers, losing is never an option. But remember that losing has less to do with the score than it does with the spirit. We can always improve the score, but we will never win if we quench the spirit of our young dreamers. No one can run with a broken spirit.

According to Your Faith

In my early years, I felt unworthy of God's attention, and that feeling became my greatest enemy. The closer I came to success, the more I sabotaged my own efforts. At first, I defined my actions as "humility"—but at the same time, I secretly disdained those who did succeed. As time went on, I realized that my definition of faith was damaging my spirit.

Jesus reminds us that genuine faith is produced by our confidence in God's ability, not trust in our own.

*And after He had come into the house, the blind men came up to Him, and Jesus said to them, "Do you believe that **I am able to do this?**" They said to Him, "Yes, Lord"* (MATT. 9:28, EMPHASIS ADDED).

The question Jesus posed to the two blind beggars is the one He asks of us today: "Do you believe that I am able to do this?" Jesus doesn't ask if you believe that *you* can do it. He asks if you believe that *God* can do it!

Do you believe that God can repair your marriage? Do you believe that God can speak through your vocal cords? Is He able to use your words to heal others? Do you believe that God can build a successful ministry or business through you? Do those whose dreams you want to release see this kind of faith in you?

Don't say something is impossible until you've done it yourself!

You can't do any of this on your own, of course — but do you believe that God can? That is the essence of a faith that will take you and your dreamers the distance.

Faith of Our Fathers

Titus Coan is one of my heroes. Through his books, he has become a coach to me. In 1837, God used this unassuming man to bring a great revival to Hawaii. He was a short, stocky fellow, living in a foreign culture among a people who spoke an unfamiliar language. Yet in a few years, the sleepy town of Hilo swelled to twice its size, simply because people longed to experience the touch of God!

One day while feeling completely inadequate and ill-equipped for what God had required of me, I visited Titus's grave on a hill near Haili church, the congregation he founded. After 10 years of pastoring, God was stirring my heart to pioneer again, and the thought scared me to death. I stood over his grave and poured out my heart to God:

> *God, I really need Your help this time. Forgive my presumption, but I know that Elisha asked for a double portion of Elijah's spirit before he was taken away. I realize that Titus Coan was taken in 1882. I guess I'm 110 years late, but I'll ask anyway. I ask for a double portion of his spirit.*
>
> *I feel about as inadequate as he must have, yet You worked in spite of him. You may need to do the same with me until I learn to believe more—but I will! I know it wasn't Titus Coan who accomplished all that took place. It was You all along, wasn't it? Would You work through me, like You did through him? Would You give me the same passion? Would You be so gracious as to show me what You showed him?*

I silently stood there for what seemed an eternity. No bright lights. No parting of the heavens. No booming voice. Yet I walked away with a renewed faith, convinced that God was able to do what He had promised.

Nearly a decade later, I remain amazed at His patience. He has always been able, even when I was not. I found that I was not waiting on God for His miracles so much as He was waiting on me to believe.

Coach, what do you believe God can do in and through you? What do you believe God can do in and through those whose dreams He wants you to help release?

Take a Moment

Identify the areas where you feel inadequate to accomplish what God is asking of you. Let Him know your fears. Write them down and make them the target of your prayers; then watch for the ways He will stretch you and convince you that *He* is able.

Dream Killer #7: Unresolved Sin

Your sins have withheld good from you.
JEREMIAH 5:25

Thieves steal thousands of cars each year in California, but in 1984, one theft dominated the radio waves and made the lead story of virtually every newscast.

Why?

A man had laced a box of crackers with poison and put them in his car, intending to take them to a rodent-plagued vacation cabin. Just as he prepared to leave, he realized that he'd forgotten something and darted back into the house, his car still idling. An unseen thief realized his opportunity and immediately stole the vehicle. When the man returned and realized what had taken place, he felt great concern — but not primarily for his stolen car. He felt most concerned for the thief, whom he feared might be tempted to help himself to the poisonous crackers still sitting on the car's front seat!

Police put out an all points bulletin to apprehend the thief. Television newscasters put the story on high priority and radio stations preempted their regular programs for this late-breaking report. Why did the authorities feel so desperate to find the car bandit? They most wanted, not to punish him, but *to save his life!*

It's not sin that destroys God's people but *unresolved* sin. God is hard on sin but for good reason. He knows how He created us and that we aren't made to prosper in sin. It's like plunging your hand into a vat of hydrochloric acid; you'll soon find out (when you pull out nothing but a stump) that your hand wasn't created to flourish in such a hostile environment. In the same way, God knows that the presence of sin eats away our futures and dissolves our potential.

God's Amazing Grace

The most powerful antidote for the venom of sin is repentance. Quick repentance breaks the grip of sin and places the believer back under the protection of God's grace. The adversary of our souls knows that the wages of sin is death, and he means to see that payroll expand. He understands how repentance appropriates God's grace; this is why he will do everything he can to keep you and your dreamers from repenting.

God's grace is not some weak-kneed, passive approach to sin. The grace of God does not ignore the devastating effects of evil. Instead, it powerfully works against hell's desire that the death sentence fall on as many as possible. God's amazing grace intercepts Satan's efforts and stems the tide of the enemy's attempt to enlarge the population of hell. With the authority of heaven, grace silences the voices that demand immediate judgment and gives guilty sinners a chance to repent.

Oh, His amazing grace!

A Dream Releaser recognizes the power of grace. He understands the deteriorating and debilitating effects of sin and refuses to ignore its consequences. Motivated out of sheer love, he cannot ignore the catastrophe of impenitence.

Hudson Taylor, one of history's most eminent missionaries, repeatedly underscored the importance of repentance. He knew that a repenting man is a healthy man, a repenting marriage is a healthy marriage and a repenting church is a healthy church. So he made it his habit to greet his coworkers with an enthusiastic, "Have you repented yet today?" He understood sin, but he *cherished* grace.

Unresolved bitterness is like drinking poison and waiting for the other person to die!

Take a Moment

With your group of young dreamers, consider the gift of accountability. Talk about sin and consider God's amazing grace. Ask for permission to speak into one another's life. No prerequisite for spiritual health is more basic than staying true to Him.

Dream Killer #8: The Inability to Act

For the dream comes through much effort.

ECCLESIASTES 5:3

Make no mistake. Dreams are never fulfilled by complacency.

God never puts a medal on laziness. Faith requires diligence. While genuine faith never results from good works, good works do indeed result from genuine faith. "I preached," said Paul, "that they should repent and turn to God and *prove their repentance by their deeds*" (Acts 26:20, *NIV*, emphasis added).

The ability to act will always be one of the greatest gifts any Dream Releaser will ever receive. No dream will come true unless we act in cooperation with God to make it come true. Remember this: Mountain-moving faith always carries a pick!

If we were walking on a hiking trail and I truly believed that a vein of gold lay under our path, what would I do? I surely wouldn't say, in holy tones, "Bless God. I *believe* (add vibrato here for effect) there's gold beneath my feet!" Then, after much ado, casually move on.

No! If I believed that gold lay under my feet, I'd yell, "Hey, I THINK THERE'S GOLD HERE! Hand me a pick! Move aside! I'm going to dig!"

Dreams, by their very nature, tend to be broad and vague. These visions and impulses must be converted into reality through specific steps of daily and weekly action points. Help your young dreamers to prioritize these steps and schedule each one into a weekly planner. Then review these plans often to make sure your dreamers are investing their efforts into fruit-bearing activities that help them stay obedient to the course God has for them.

Mountain-moving faith always carries a pick!

Many years ago, I had a dream to reach people for Christ and to shepherd God's flock. But if my dream were to come true, I realized that I had to become a master communicator of simple truths from God's Word.

I had sat under many messages that gave me more indigestion than insight. My frustration grew as I traveled from church to church, looking for someone who would feed me. I knew the transforming power of God's Word, but somehow I wasn't being transformed.

I needed a plan. I had to start reading the Bible for myself until its message permeated every dark corner in me. I couldn't hold others responsible to spoon-feed me; I had to feed myself.

I devised a plan to break the Bible into daily readings that would take me through the Bible each year. I then put together a journal, so I could keep myself account-able by putting into action what God was teaching me.

Over the last 12 years, this method has proven its worth. Many others, including pastors, business people and youth, have used this daily devotional method to increase their depth and love for God's Word.

A clear, methodical approach will help you (and your young dreamers) to move steadily closer to the person God designed you to be. This is a cooperative effort between you and God. He wants to work in tandem with you. Share your approach with a spouse or friend and ask them to help you. But the key is to *take action!*

Little happens apart from a dream; but without a concise plan and the ability to take action, that dream will remain just a dream—and only the graveyard will benefit from its compelling vision.

The heights by great men reached and kept Were not attained by sudden flight, But they while their companions slept Were toiling upward in the night.

HENRY WADSWORTH LONGFELLOW, "THE LADDER OF SAINT AUGUSTINE"

Keep Tapping on the Cage

Decide now to take nothing with you when you die. Leave it all behind. Dream killers will oppose you and your dreamers, demanding that you hoard it all for yourselves. Resist them. Fight them. Defeat them. And through faith in the risen Son of God, keep tapping on the cage until those dreams—and those who dream them—take flight.

Take a Moment

Get your group together. If you haven't started already, start doing devotions together, always remembering that any journey begins with the first step. What is your first step? Write it down and prioritize it into your schedule. Fight the tendency to procrastinate. Soon you will be able to look back and see what God can do from just one step. (You can obtain a devotional starter kit on the Web at www.eNewhope.org.)

. . . .

Chapter Eight

KEYS OF A DREAM RELEASER

*I have a key in my bosom, called Promise, that will, I am
persuaded, open any lock in Doubting Castle.*

JOHN BUNYAN, *PILGRIM'S PROGRESS*

*I*t's not always easy to locate the keys that unlock the doors to someone's potential. I have found some individuals reticent and others unwilling.

Nevertheless, you cannot allow the resistance of a few to dictate the urgency of your call. Even Jesus had a Judas—yet in John 13:2-5, we find Jesus washing the feet of His betrayer. The master chose to put on a towel instead of an air. He picked up a basin instead of a grudge. He refused to use Judas's weakness as fodder for retaliation.

The final step in your becoming a Dream Releaser lies in your ability to be trusted. You must become a steward of the keys God commends to you. Your faithfulness with this trust will dictate both the breadth of your mantle and the strength of your legacy.

Just as talent can be either invested or consumed, so too keys can either open a door or lock someone out. These keys come with options. They will test your ability to make wise, selfless choices—the greatest test of all.

Consider three keys that the Lord entrusts to each of His Dream Releasers.

Key #1: Stewarding Influence

*Let your light shine before men in such a way that they may **see** your **good works**, and **glorify your Father** who is in heaven.*

MATTHEW 5:16, EMPHASIS ADDED

The influential pastor of a large church became disheartened and depressed. All the efforts of a close friend to encourage him met with failure. At a point of desperation, the disenchanted leader lamented, "I just feel like jumping off a building!"

"Go ahead," his friend replied, "and a thousand people will follow you."

As a Dream Releaser, God entrusts you with an increasing amount of influence. If stewarded well, it can command armies, move nations, right injustices and transform lives. If abused, it can corrupt even the greatest of causes. The book of Galatians gives us great insight into this gift of influence and how it can be both used and abused.

God directed Paul to take the gospel to the Gentiles, while He assigned Peter to take the same message to his skeptical countrymen, the Jewish people. In order to fully equip these couriers of the message, the Lord gave each a measure of influence to break through the disbelief of the unconvinced.

Galatians 2:11-13 tells what happened to Peter in Antioch. Skeptical Jews and inquiring Gentiles had gathered for an evening meal, and although Peter had earlier spoken freely to both groups, peer pressure pushed him to fraternize with the Jews while refusing to mix with Gentiles. And so Paul the apostle confronted him:

> *But when Peter came to Antioch, I had to oppose him publicly, speaking strongly against what he was doing, for it was very wrong. When he first arrived, he ate with the Gentile Christians. . . . But afterward, when some Jewish friends of James came, Peter wouldn't eat with the Gentiles anymore because he was afraid of what these legalists would say.* **Then the other Jewish Christians followed Peter's hypocrisy, and even Barnabas was influenced to join them** (*NLT*, EMPHASIS ADDED).

Even Barnabas—the son of encouragement, the man of great mercy—was "influenced" by Peter to compromise and concede to error. The apostle's God-given influence had a far-reaching impact.

It's easy to get seduced by your influence to open doors, gain personal favors and be noticed. But such influence, like milk left out, can quickly sour.

A few years ago, I had to make one of the most difficult decisions of my life. After 12 years of ministry, I felt a divine discontent that drove me to a season of inquiry. After months of agony, I felt nearly certain that I was to move to the capitol island, 200 miles away, and pioneer again. The decision would carry huge implications. It meant relocating my children during their high school years. It would require us to sell our home and leave relationships we had built up over more than a decade.

It is wisdom to use your influence. It is criminal to sell it.

ED COLE

I began the slow and painful process of notifying key people of my growing conviction. I identified a dozen couples whom I wanted to inform privately before the news went public—people of influence, not only in the congregation, but also in my personal life.

One couple, a retired contractor and his wife, had taken their place among our dearest friends. Marie was like a mother to me and a grandmother to our children. She and her husband, Calvin, lived in a coastal town and drove nearly an hour each way to get to church. One Sunday after services, I arrived home to find them waiting in our driveway. I approached their car and began to describe the new ministry direction. At first, Marie insisted that I reassess the situation; it was obviously an untimely move. I hesitated because I knew of their love for me. If they saw a red flag, I knew I couldn't proceed.

Just then, Marie began to weep. I felt confused and asked her what was wrong. "The selfish part of me wants you to reconsider," she said, "but I know that what you are hearing is of God. And when He confirms something in me, I can't help but cry. You have equated risk, not with the fear of failure, but with pleasing God, and that delights His heart. You are taking a great risk by starting all over again, and because of that, God is poised to do something great."

The influence of Marie's words added the weight I needed in the keel of my decision. Her influence galvanized the confidence I required to head out into the open ocean. Her influence, unselfishly stewarded in my life, brought a buoyancy that God used to launch the new work.

How you exercise the gift of influence will determine your legacy. Steward your influence well.

Take a Moment
Reflect. Where has God given you influence in your home, church, work or school? In whose life have you been given that great privilege? How are you stewarding it? Consider a few ways to build your influence:

- Begin praying for those in your sphere of influence.

- Ask God to give you specific words of encouragement for these men and women.
- Ask for specific Scriptures that would inspire their faith.

Key #2: Stewarding Authority

For this reason I am writing these things while absent,
in order that when present I may not use severity,
*in accordance with **the authority which the Lord gave me,***
for building up and not for tearing down.

2 CORINTHIANS 13:10, EMPHASIS ADDED

God entrusts every Dream Releaser with a measure of authority. He wants you to use this authority to release dreams that would otherwise remain stranded on distant shores.

Authority is a God-entrusted gift that grows out of a trustworthy and consistent lifestyle. It adds weight to words, confidence to counsel and credence to correction. Authority stewarded true to God's intent can demolish doubt and hasten receptivity. No Dream Releaser can function without it.

Authority has been sorely misunderstood in our culture of private parking spaces, personal favors and inside privileges. Stewarded well, authority can yield amazing results. Abused, it can destroy a life or ruin a whole generation.

Why does God give us such a powerful gift to steward? Paul tells the Corinthians that the Lord gave him apostolic authority "for building you up, not for tearing you down" (2 Corinthians 13:10, *NIV*).

Let this truth sink deep into your soul. The reason that God entrusts Dream Releasers with authority is not to build themselves up but to build *others* up! Authority is a servant's tool, not a leader's weapon.

This distinction means a lot to me, for I came close to abusing this gift. If not for the help of a friend, I might well have derailed a man's journey to God.

Milton served as our volunteer sound man. He had worked professionally for such well-known entertainers as Don Ho, and experts widely considered him one of Hawaii's best. Although he wasn't a Christian, our music director asked him to assist us in our Easter services, to be held in a 10,000-seat basketball arena. In such a huge place it would take a miracle of electronic proportions just to control the sound! We expected 6,000 attendees at each of three services, so we had to be ready.

We rented the necessary truss systems, lights and speakers, to the tune of $24,000—no small outlay of cash. At our first service on Saturday night, an annoying hiss began in the speakers. By the time I got up to preach, it had grown into a mighty rushing wind (minus the Holy Spirit). I tried my best to keep calm, but I'm sure my frustration bled through, especially when I thought of how much this electronic windstorm was costing us.

The Lord was gracious and many came to faith that evening, but still I felt upset. As soon as the service ended, I scuttled my first option (murder) in favor of giving our sound man a piece of my mind. As I descended in wrath from the platform, my music director caught up with me.

"I know it killed you tonight, battling the interference," he said, "but I just want you to know that as much as you suffered, Milton suffered a hundred times more. He so wanted to correct the hiss, but that wasn't possible without shutting down all the amps and replacing the faulty one. He felt so helpless. He couldn't do a thing except hurt with you the whole service."

I have never felt anger melt away so quickly. I walked up to Milton, who braced himself for a reprimand. Instead, I threw my arms around him and thanked him for hurting with me. I felt horrible for him. Especially with his experience and ability, it must have felt like his worst nightmare. I thanked him for his heart and reminded him that God still did His work, despite the distraction. Tears welled up in his eyes.

I've never seen someone so motivated to remedy a problem. He stayed past 2:00 A.M. until the owner of the rental company brought in a replacement amp (the call didn't go out until midnight!). Milton later gave his heart to Christ; a year later we hired him on staff.

And that Easter, 1,100 men and women opened their hearts to Christ.

What do you think? Maybe that "mighty rushing wind" was more than an electronic windstorm.

I shudder to imagine the devastating effect my misguided authority could have caused. My scathing rebuke would have crushed Milton's spirit and driven him further away from making a decision for Christ.

God feels no reticence about giving His Dream Releasers more authority if they will use it for what He intended. He never designed authority for our own purposes, nor did He give it to us to use to degrade others who don't match up to our expectations.

Want to know the easiest way to gain more authority? Start building someone up! When God sees you using authority for His purposes, He will be delighted to increase the supply.

Take a Moment

Consider young Joshua, a novice leader in the worst of circumstances. God's plan called for him to lead the next generation of Hebrews into the Promised Land.

Hear God's instructions to the people in Deuteronomy 1:38: "Joshua the son of Nun, who stands before you, he shall enter there; *encourage him*, for he shall cause Israel to inherit it." Potential Joshuas stand all around you, if you'll only see them.

Make a prayer list of several individuals in whom you see potential. Perhaps you have seen glimpses of their gifts or, from time to time, have seen them show promise. Write down their names and ask God to give you a word that might nudge them into flight. Challenge them to meet with you once a week. Young, emerging leaders feast off of sincere encouragement!

Key #3: Stewarding Problems

It is not the healthy who need a doctor, but the sick. I have not come to call the righteous, but sinners.

MARK 2:17, *NIV*

If you are to become a Dream Releaser, God must first be able to entrust to you the problems of the kingdom.

Problems? That's right! The people of God come rid-
dled with problems. We have problems in our families,
problems in our leadership, problems in our marriages,
problems in our faith, problems in our . . . We face problems in just about every area of life. No one, of course,
likes to face problems; we'd rather they simply disappear.

When God asks for volunteers to receive the blessings of the kingdom, mobs line up for blocks around, like
movie fans hoping to purchase tickets to a popular film.
Books and seminars offer techniques to help us
get what we want—with greater speed
and less pain. We love it when God
lavishes on us all the wonderful
advantages due His children. We
turn Bible promises into mantras. We remind God that
He's supposed to bless us. We believe by faith that those
blessings are ours. We repeat affirmations ad infinitum.

But what happens when God hands out problems?
That line remains sparse and unattended. While the
blessings line stays packed, the problems line looks nearly empty. At the head of the problems line, however, you
can hear an auctioneer's voice pleading above the din:

> *"I have a single man with some minor disabili-
> ties. His record has a few blemishes, but his
> heart is good and he has great potential. He*

just needs a friend to help. Any takers?"

No response.

"No? OK. . . maybe this next one will hold more appeal. I have a young man with a great leadership gift, but pride has begun to corrode his future. He's awkward and a bit headstrong, but his latest setback has softened his heart. He needs a patient coach, a mentor. He can't do it alone, but with a little help he will amaze you. Anyone?"

No response.

"OK, let's try this one. I need someone who will help me bring hope to a small church on the west side of town. This assignment was given to a novice pastor, but right now he feels too young and doesn't have what it takes. He just needs someone to believe in him. Anyone?"

Still no takers.

This fictitious scene is not as contrived as it seems. The problems described did abound and the auctioneer is real. You can read about the first of these "unwanted assignments" in Galatians 4:13-15; his name is Paul. The second is Peter, who met Jesus again on the shores of Galilee in John 21. The third is a timid young pastor named Timothy, whom Paul encourages in 1 Timothy 4:12.

All around us live a young Paul, a brash Peter, an unsure Timothy—as well as young Priscillas, Marthas and Lydias—but until we develop the heart of a Dream Releaser, we won't see them. These great men and women often come disguised in awkward wrappings and unattractive packages. Problems beset them, but Dream Releasers can see through the unsightly wrappings.

They know that treasure hides within each one!

From a Different Perspective

When my son, Aaron, was learning the game of baseball, he graduated from T-Ball to Coach Pitch. In the new league, each team's coach pitched to his own players. The theory went that young batters would more quickly overcome their fears if a pitched baseball came as a friendly lob, rather than as an enemy fastball.

We had but one slight problem: Our coach was the worst pitcher in the league. His throws often careened off the plate and the boys had to try their luck at hitting the ball on second bounce. Several times, his pitches veered off the mark and hit one of our own batters.

To make matters worse, his placement of players on the field seemed no better than his misguided screwballs. Some of our kids would rather chase toads than fetch a ball hit in their direction. Our first baseman, a girl, seemed as afraid of the ball as we were of our pitcher.

So I organized a mutiny.

One Saturday, I gathered the parents together. After the game we planned to present our complaints to the commissioner. Not only did we fear for our kids' lives, but we also wondered how much fun can you have trying after every game to explain to your kids that a score of 30 to 1 isn't all that bad?

Just prior to the contest in question, the coach asked if any parents knew how to keep score. I volunteered. I took the score book and climbed the familiar stairs that led to the scorekeeper's box. Soon the game began, with predictable results. Our coach started the inning by striking out two of our own batters. He hit the third— which at least put a man on first—but struck out the fourth. And then we took the field, complete with toad chasers and a paranoid first base-person.

Next to the score book, I kept a running list of the coach's shortcomings as evidence for the commissioner. As the game dragged on, my shopping list of indictments mushroomed. Finally, the game mercifully ended. Armed with my evidence, I made my way down the metal staircase, toward the waiting parents poised for the overthrow. I descended the stairs, clutching my proof of our coach's inadequacy. I felt smug, like an attorney with all the evidence needed to send a man's coaching career to Death Row.

But something happened on the way to the dugout. God intercepted me in the stairwell—and like the angel who confronted Balaam, He had a drawn sword in hand. I knew He meant business!

In that moment of time, God convened His own trial.

"When was the last time you organized the parents to assist in any of the practices? Did you ever volunteer to help with the pitching, or did you just grumble?"

The sad truth was, not once did any of us offer our help in positioning the kids. Nor did we ever volunteer our assistance at practice. If we had coached our kids to catch baseballs as well as they nabbed toads, we'd unquestionably be league champions. Instead, we had spent our energy compiling errors, rather than solving them.

Then the Lord reminded me that the faults of the coach had not been exposed but *entrusted* to me—not in order to organize a takeover, but in order to mobilize the parents' involvement.

The Lord's final piece of instruction has echoed in my heart for years: *"If I cannot trust you with what I reveal, then I will no longer be able show you the hurts of My children. You will have disqualified yourself from any involvement in My plan to restore them."*

We tend to see others' blunders as their Achilles' heel. Their weakness becomes our strength. Their fallibility becomes our advantage. We wait for the best time to play our trump card—for our benefit.

Inside every one of us is a Pharisee just waiting to grow up.

James 2:13 reminds us, "For judgment will be merciless to one who has shown no mercy; mercy triumphs over judgment." God had been inviting me into His program of restoration, and I had remained blind to it. My own lack of compassion was about to disqualify me!

I can't adequately express how convicted I felt. I immediately scrapped the revolt. And though we didn't come away as champions that year, we did unburden ourselves of grumbling parent-spectators. We all joined in, and the rest of the season turned into a joyous family affair. The coach's pitching didn't improve much—but I'm happy to report that we didn't lose one kid the entire season!

We can choose whether we will view life as a film critic or as a physician. A film critic evaluates a movie in order to pass judgment. A physician inspects a patient's condition in order to bring health. A doctor locates a problem in order to bring healing. A movie reviewer locates a miscue in order to bring a verdict.

Dream Releasers always choose mercy over judgment.

Take a Moment

Think about some problems God has entrusted to you. It could be someone's shortcomings, or it could be a leader's weaknesses. Now ask God what He wants you to do. How does He want you to steward that which He has entrusted to you?

- Intercede?
- Offer help?
- Lovingly confront?

One thing for sure—He has not shown you problems in order to encourage you to gripe!

Enjoying Christmas All Year 'Round

When a Dream Releaser wisely stewards problems, influence and authority, he or she unlocks the potential bound up in young hearts. But those keys will unlock more than potential; they will also unlock the Dream Releaser's joy. Using the keys to open my door gets me in; but when I open someone else's, that's when God walks in!

One Christmas, Abby, our youngest, was only five but already well on her way to understanding Christmastime competition with two older siblings.

We have a family tradition to open one gift each on Christmas Eve. The rest of our presents must wait till Christmas morn. Each year my children had to endure a night of restless anticipation and their father's lectures about delayed gratification.

Finally, Christmas morning dawned in its all-too-tardy fashion. Our three children had positioned themselves around our proud Noble fir, a merry evergreen festooned with popcorn strands and "one part glitter, five parts glue" ornaments they had handmade in art class.

Abby launched the first attack on the neatly wrapped targets, closely followed by Amy and Aaron. I delighted in the joyful chaos as I sipped a cup of coffee, watching my children enjoy Christmas.

Every year at the apex of the battle, my wife would prompt the children with a stern directive: "Write down who gave what, so you can send thank-you cards!" That was her yearly mantra, followed by groans and comments about having already thrown away the tags. "Then start now," she'd say, "and from now on, make sure you write down the rest of them!" The children would begrudgingly oblige and hastily scribble down names and addresses. (My wife doesn't give up easily. I should know; she married me.)

Then they continued the assault on any unopened survivors.

I'm usually the last to open my gifts, and for some reason, this particular year I had received several more presents than usual. When the feeding frenzy subsided, I found myself with about a dozen unopened packages.

You might think I'd feel elated over the inequality — but this year it had an opposite effect. Perhaps it was a sign of age, but opening my own gifts had lost much of its appeal. Maybe it's a father thing, but the dilemma had me stumped. How could it be? I was taking more pleasure in watching my children open their gifts than I did from unwrapping my own!

My three children, like forlorn orphans peering through a bakery window, stared at my unopened gifts. With a little imagination, our living room could have made a perfect set for *David Copperfield*.

"Hey, I know!" I said with a start. "Let's have each of you open four presents each! What do you think?"

They shrieked, and the scene shifted from a David Copperfield scene to a blue-light special. The room exploded with excitement as wrapping paper, like colored shrapnel, began flying everywhere. Just then, my wife's voice rose above the sound of ripping tissue and tearing cardboard: "Write down who gave what, so you can send thank-you cards!"

That's how Dream Releasers feel. Like parents, they experience greater joy in the success of a loved one than in their own achievements. They love to encourage; they understand that problems will surface, but they do not fear them.

The influence of a Dream Releaser, mixed with generous helpings of love, can cut through the thickest fog and give renewed confidence. And the best thing of all?

For a Dream Releaser, Christmas happens all year 'round.

. . . .

Chapter Nine

PORTRAIT OF A DREAM RELEASER

"Keep, ancient lands, your storied pomp!" cries she
With silent lips. "Give me your tired, your poor,
Your huddled masses yearning to breathe free,
The wretched refuse of your teeming shore.
Send these, the homeless, tempest-tossed to me.
I lift my lamp beside the golden door."

EMMA LAZARUS,
"THE NEW COLOSSUS," 1883

*O*ver a century has passed since Emma Lazarus wrote her famous poem. Since that time, thousands of immigrants have passed under the shadow of the Statue of Liberty. The copper lady is an invitation to hope, a summons to new vistas, new horizons and new seasons.

I believe this poem should adorn the walls of every church, every home and every office. Its spirit has built our nation, and its spirit will build it still. Our homes and churches fairly burst with caged birds yearning to "breathe free."

Emma Lazarus paints a stunning portrait of a Dream Releaser, one who not only invites but who also nudges dreams to fly. The beauty of Dream Releasers begins at the heart and bleeds into everything they do and say.

The Heart of a Dream Releaser

The one who does not love does not know God, for God is love.
1 JOHN 4:8

God's heart beats for His people, and that's why the Bible says that God is love. Love creates a greenhouse effect that allows life to flourish. It produces an atmosphere in which dreams can be released.

That's what happened with an Old Testament character named Joseph. I noticed something intriguing about this young man. His father, Jacob, made no bones about the fact that he loved Joseph more than all of his other sons:

> *Now Israel loved Joseph more than any of his other sons, because he had been born to him in his old age; and he made a richly ornamented robe for him. [Now] Joseph had a dream* (GEN. 37:3,5, *NIV*).

Joseph was the only son that Jacob really loved— *and he was also the only one able to dream.* Coincidence? I don't think so. Something about the assurance of being loved allows a person to dream, to uncover hidden potential. Love awakens the faith to believe. First John 4:18 reminds us that "perfect love casts out fear."

Jacob's love released Joseph to be a dreamer. Love built an atmosphere in which the young man could freely hear God's plans for his future. And unknown to his brothers, within this spoiled dreamer God had hidden the deliverance of Israel.

Love can set dreams free, while its absence leaves dreamers "yearning to breathe free."

Many years ago a reporter from the *New York Times* interviewed Marilyn Monroe. The reporter knew of Marilyn's past and how in her early years the actress had been shuffled from one foster home to another. The reporter asked the celebrity, "Did you ever feel loved by any of the foster families with whom you lived?"

"Once," Marilyn replied, "when I was about seven or eight. The woman I was living with was putting on her makeup, and I was watching her. She was in a happy mood, so she reached over and patted my cheeks with her rouge puff . . . and for that moment, I felt loved by her."

Tears rolled down Marilyn Monroe's face as she remembered this long-ago incident. Why? The touch lasted only a few seconds — but that seemingly insignificant act felt to her like pouring buckets of love on a parched life. Only a few years later, Marilyn Monroe shuffled through multiple marriages and ended her life as a suicide.

Love's absence can shrivel potential like the Sahara sun; but when it lifts its golden lamp, dreams begin to blossom, even in the most adverse conditions.

Creating a Climate for Dreams

A few summers ago, my family and I visited Tennessee, where I spoke at a local church. It's a beautiful state, despite its blistering heat. They say that you're a true

Tennesseean only if you are still standing at the end of summer. It is hot!

We chose to stay a few nights in the Grand Ole Opry Hotel, an immense facility. I had no idea of the sheer expanse of this indoor city—nearly 15 acres under one roof.

More amazing still, the flora and fauna on the inside resembles that of Hawaii. Its temperature and humidity-controlled environment allow even tropical flowers to bloom. But open a door to the outside and it feels like you're checking your turkey on Thanksgiving Day.

It intrigued me that plants that on the outside would be dying, on the inside were thriving. What should have been floundering was flourishing!

That's exactly what genuine love does. It builds a greenhouse effect in families and in relationships. What normally would die will thrive, and what ordinarily would wither will blossom. Unconditional love, freely expressed, builds greenhouses for young dreamers.

Greenhouses are built with words. Genuine expressions of interest and constant reminders of His promises erect cultures in which dreams thrive.

Greenhouses are destroyed by words. Rash judgments tear down futures, one hope at a time.

Take a Moment

Rate yourself on a scale of 1 to 10 (with 10 as the highest mark) for each of the following:

1. How would a person rate my ability to build a culture of love?

   1   2   3   4   5   6   7   8   9   1 0

2. I enjoy people and seeing them succeed. I do not use them to fulfill my goals.

   1   2   3   4   5   6   7   8   9   1 0

The Mouth of a Dream Releaser

"Sticks and stones may break my bones, but words can never harm me." Those words might make up a children's rhyme, but they lie. Words *can* harm us. How many times do we have to see to believe?

Remember the greenhouse of love? We build such greenhouses with words. Genuine expressions of interest and constant reminders of God's promises create an environment in which dreams thrive. We also destroy greenhouses through words. Rash judgments tear down futures, one hope at a time.

Crude words drive dreams into remission because hearts are fragile. Proverbs 18:21 reminds us, "Death and life are in the power of the tongue." Sometimes I overhear an angry parent blurt out to a wayward child, "You'll never amount to anything!" Such words have buried more potential than all the wars ever fought.

Legions of fears about tomorrow often lurk in the hearts of young dreamers, stealing the confidence they so desperately need. Our words have the power to banish those ghosts. There is a force in our words that can begin to transform a life. God is looking for people who will steward words in such a way that they usher in new seasons and new beginnings.

You've Got to Say It!

> *Better is open rebuke than love that is concealed.*
> PROVERBS 27:5

No one likes to be rebuked, especially in public. It's humiliating and embarrassing. Yet the Bible reveals something we regularly fail to do that wreaks the same amount of pain: *concealing our love!*

To conceal our love for people is worse in God's eyes than the pain of being rebuked before our peers. People are desperate to feel valued. When we conceal our love, we starve them from what they need the most. How often have we condemned those who rebuke others in public, even as we withheld words of love?

Imagine that everyone you meet has hanging around his or her neck a sign that reads "Please help me to feel valuable today."

Consider a few ways that a Dream Releaser can use his or her words to express love:

- **Look for ways to give genuine encouragement.** Encouragement inspires people to attempt something wonderful.
- **Give prophetic inspiration.** Prompt young dreamers in their attempts to serve God. Speak specific promises that remind them of God's ability.
- **Ask God for the "tongue of a disciple."** Why? "That I may know how to sustain the weary one with a word" (Isa. 50:4).
- **Ask God for "the tongue of the wise"** (Prov. 12:18). Wise words bring healing.

Years ago I heard a story called "The Whisper Test." It tells about a Dream Releaser named Ms. Leonard. Here's the story as I remember it:

I grew up knowing I was different. I was born with a cleft palate, and when I started school, my classmates made it clear to me how I looked to others. When my school-mates asked me, "What hap-pened to your lip?" I would always tell them that I fell and cut it on a piece of glass. Somehow, it seemed more acceptable to have suffered an accident than to have been born different. I was convinced that no one out-side my family could love me.

There was, however, a teacher in the second grade whom we all adored: Ms. Leonard. She was short, round and happy. She was a sparkling lady.

Annually, we'd have to take a hearing test. Ms. Leonard gave the test to everyone in the class. And now, finally, it was my turn. I knew from the past years that as we stood against the door and covered one ear, the teacher sitting at her desk would whisper something, and we would have to repeat it back. She'd whisper things like "The sky is blue" or "Do you have new shoes?"

I stood against the door with one ear covered and waited there for the words that God must have put in her mouth, seven words that changed my life. Ms. Leonard said in a whisper:

"I wish you were my little girl."

I didn't know what to say, and even if I did, I wouldn't have been able to say anything. I tried repeating it, but I was crying too hard. So she repeated it again.

I guess by my tears she knew that I heard; and that day, I passed the greatest test of all—knowing that I was chosen and someone loved me.

That's what all Dream Releasers do. They use the power of words to illuminate God's heart. They choose words that serve as excellent conductors, because that causes young dreams to glow.

Take a Moment

Rate yourself for each of the following:

1. I am known as an encourager, never as a skeptic.

    1   2   3   4   5   6   7   8   9   1 0

2. I am expressive with words of love and appreciation for others.

    1   2   3   4   5   6   7   8   9   1 0

The Eyes of a Dream Releaser

Love cares more for others than for self. . . .
Doesn't keep score of the sins of others, . . .
always looks for the best.

1 CORINTHIANS 13:4-5,7,
THE MESSAGE

We usually see what we look for. Maybe we've never noticed a certain make of car; but once we decide that's the model we want, we begin to see it everywhere. If I look for people with pimples, I'll find a world badly in need of antibiotics. If I look for faults, I will discover what a wretched society we live in.

In the same way, those who believe that everyone has a God-given dream just waiting to be released will see a world full of wonderful potential.

The great composer Ludwig Von Beethoven became deaf in his later years. Although stricken with useless ears, Beethoven continued to create new compositions on a harpsichord badly out of tune. Several strings on his instrument had broken, while the remaining ones had long since lost their best voices. Yet, hour after hour, tears streamed down his face as he played.

To anyone with ears to hear, the performance sounded discordant and dissonant. But not to Beethoven! He heard the sound that the instrument *should* make, not the sound that it *did* make.

In the same way, train your eyes to see future potential, rather than current condition. Look for evidence of God's presence, rather than for proof of His absence. Listen for the finished symphony. Hear the refined masterpiece.

Jeremiah 15:19 gives us a glimpse from heaven's curriculum for building Dream Releasers. "If you extract the precious from the worthless," it says, "you will become My spokesman." Each time I read this passage, I remember that something precious lies in everything, even if it seems utterly useless.

Seeing What Others Could Not

It was December 8, 1983, and the temperature plummeted below freezing. An 11-year-old boy sat watching television in his suburban Philadelphia home, preoccupied with the evening news. A report highlighted the plight of the homeless in Philadelphia and the real risk of freezing to death overnight.

The news bothered Trevor Ferrell. This was something he had never considered.

Suddenly, a thought triggered in his young mind. He had little need of a blanket in his warm suburban home. Why not give it to a homeless person and keep him from freezing during the frigid wintry night? The solution seemed so simple.

The young crusader quickly went to his room, gathered his blanket and a pillow from his bed and headed off into the night, determined to find a homeless person.

Trevor's parents, Frank and Janet, naturally refused to let their preadolescent venture into the cold evening alone. But their son's determination soon convinced them to help. Frank loaded the family car with a single blanket, pillow and an 11-year-old filled with resolve, and father and son headed for the streets. Little did they realize their trek would forever change, not only the Ferrell family, but the city of Philadelphia.

From the warmth of the car, Trevor spotted a homeless man curling up over a steam grate, bracing himself to face the frigid night. The boy asked his father to stop, grabbed the blanket and pillow and, without a word, handed them to the shivering man alone in the dark. The eyes of the homeless man met Trevor's and the shivering man uttered three simple words that would touch a young boy's heart:

"God bless you."

Trevor could hardly contain his excitement. The next night he insisted on going back out with more blankets.

Soon, the Ferrell household ran out of blankets and pillows. So Trevor began to enlist the aid of his neighborhood friends. One mother called Trevor's mother to complain.

"Do you know that your son has convinced my boy to give away all of our blankets?" she said, obviously frustrated.

"I'm not surprised," Trevor's mother wryly responded. "Last night he gave away my winter coat!"

Word began to spread of the 11-year-old boy on a mission of mercy with Philadelphia's homeless. The local news ran several stories about Trevor's outreach. Soon, help and aid began pouring in from every quarter.

A group of fraternity and sorority students from a local college volunteered to help. A fast-food chain provided food. One person donated a van. A supply officer from nearby Fort Dix called to say the U.S. Army had a warehouse full of surplus blankets and a couple of hundred coats that Trevor could have for his mission. Before long, the whole city was abuzz with talk of young Trevor's campaign.

Unfortunately, great efforts attract not only supporters but also skeptics. City leaders, somewhat embarrassed that an 11-year-old was calling so much attention to their homeless problem, convened a seminar of experts to address the topic. Trevor received an invitation to join the panel. At one point, a local professor of sociology was asked to comment on Trevor's approach to the homeless problem. Clearing his throat, he began his scholarly opinion.

"Homelessness," he said in a deep voice, "is a complex problem. Trevor is providing simplistic answers. However, complex problems require complex solutions."

The moderator then turned to Trevor and asked what he thought of this comment.

"I don't really know," the young man replied. "I'm just a kid. But tonight when I'm giving out blankets, I'll ask the people whether they would rather have my blankets or his complex solutions."

The efforts of this one amazing young boy reached as far as Calcutta, India, where Mother Teresa felt so moved that she asked for Trevor to visit her work on two separate occasions.

And how did this all begin? At first glance, it would seem that Trevor Ferrell was quite an exceptional young man. Not so. In almost every respect, Trevor was an ordinary kid, a shy and unassuming kind of boy.

Yet he had a Dream Releaser disguised as a Sunday School teacher.

A few weeks prior to his first trek into the city, a Sunday School teacher told each child that God had a dream for each of them, but that dream would come unassembled. "Be watching," she said, "because God will reveal what He has for you to do."

Trevor had the courage to believe that God could do exceedingly more through him than he could ever imagine. That dream continues today, with over 2 million meals served and more than 1,800 formerly homeless people receiving permanent housing through Trevor's efforts.

And perhaps most significantly, since 1983, *no one* has frozen to death on the streets of Philadelphia.

The assignment of a Dream Releaser always begins very simply. No programs. No campaigns. It begins when you pick up a blanket and pillow and walk into the night.

Take a Moment
Rate yourself for each of the following:

1. I always look for the good in others.

   1   2   3   4   5   6   7   8   9   1 0

2. I never settle for quick conclusions, and I take the time to see things from the other person's perspective.

   1   2   3   4   5   6   7   8   9   1 0

Take Action

Improve something about yourself today. Write down how you will focus on making personal changes during the next three weeks. Even if you improve just 1 percent a day, by the end of the year you will have improved more than *300 percent!*

Chapter Ten

CALLING ALL DREAM RELEASERS

*M*illions of dreams lie captive in the hearts of men and women all around us. Each has a dream of what he or she can be for God. This dream, divinely wired into their souls, holds the blueprint for their God-given assignment. It contains their passion, their potential, their destiny.

This dream may see them making a difference in the world or having a God-glorifying family. The dream may be to have a business based on principles of integrity, to have a ministry that will change lives or to rear children in the ways of God. But whatever the dream may be, the capacity to fulfill it lies within each of their hearts.

But like a caged bird, those dreams remain imprisoned.

Just imagine what could happen if those dreams were released. Imagine what could happen in our churches, in our families, in our communities!

Tapping on Cages

Her name was Grace Flint. She challenged me to be a Dream Releaser.

I received Christ when I was 19 and I immediately ignited for God. The day I became a Christian, a Campus Crusade counselor gave me a *Living New Testament*. Three months later, I felt the unmistakable call to enter full-time ministry. Now with my trusty paperback Bible and John 3:16 memorized, I was armed and dangerous. I enrolled in Bible college, high on zeal and low on knowledge.

I well remember the first day of class. The teacher introduced a short devotional by saying, "Let's all turn to Jeremiah."

I had no idea who Jeremiah was. Eager to meet this new student, I spun my chair around. From the snickering of the other students, I knew I had missed something.

"In your Bible, Wayne," came a condescending voice from a smug kid sitting next to me. "Turn to Jeremiah . . . in your Bible!"

With only a New Testament in my possession, his advice didn't help much. I spent the whole period looking for Jeremiah in my worn paperback. I sighed with relief when the class ended. I quickly left, embarrassed, and questioned my readiness for the school year ahead.

The next class, however—Bible history taught by Dr. Grace Flint—quelled my doubts. While Dr. Flint had earned a reputation as a brilliant scholar, it wasn't her scholarship that I remember most.

I remember her as a tough-as-nails Dream Releaser.

Our homework assignments could not be turned in handwritten; they had to be typed. Remember, the computer revolution hadn't yet occurred by the early '70s. We had no Macs, no Dells, no Compaq laptops. The only thing IBM had to offer was an electric typewriter with a tube of white out filling in for the delete key.

I recall getting back my first assignment from Sister Flint (as we respectfully addressed her) with my grade noticeably missing. In its place was a handwritten note. I slowly read the first of many gifts that became increasingly valuable to me:

Thank you for being in my class, Wayne. Your insight and contribution was so refreshing during our discussion time. Your obvious zeal for Christ inspires us all. I look with great anticipation for how God will use you for His purposes. The Kingdom of God awaits you!

I felt so inspired; I must have read and reread that last line a dozen times before lights-out that evening. It was as if God had dialed extra reverb into that phrase, just for me.

"The Kingdom of God awaits you."

I took every class Dr. Flint taught, not because I liked Bible history, but because I so desperately needed to hear the words of a Dream Releaser. On every paper she would scribble a handwritten note that gradually helped to unlock my potential.

"The Kingdom of God awaits you."

This was Sister Flint's way of saying "I believe in you"—and she tapped my cage and nudged my dreams into flight.

Hearing Heaven's Trumpet Call

God is issuing a call for Dream Releasers.

Whether you are a parent, pastor, youth worker, uncle, aunt, business leader, teacher or social worker, your greatest contribution depends upon your response to this invitation.

Will you sign up to be a Dream Releaser? Will you ask God to develop your heart, your eyes and your mouth to release the dreams that remain locked inside so many others? This world is crying out for Dream Releasers.

I invite you to pray the following prayer. But I must caution you: it *will* change your life!

Lord Jesus, make me like You. Please give me the wisdom to serve Your people well. Help me to begin to truly serve You, starting today. For

*up to now, I really have done nothing. Make
me a Dream Releaser. I am done with living
for myself alone. Grant me the insight necessary to lead others through the roadblocks that
hinder them from becoming all they were meant
to be. I give You full use of my life for Your
purposes and I will steward the trust You have
given me. In the name of Him who created
dreams to be fulfilled. Amen.*

Entering the Joy of Your Master

Watch a tennis match at Wimbledon. Often the cameras scan the gallery and pause on a contestant's family. The huddled group in the bleachers mirrors the emotions of their son or daughter on the court. They feel every miss and exult in every point. It's no longer just another person on the court. *They* are on the court together, alternately aching or rejoicing with every loss or gain. The parents take as much, if not more, joy in their child's victory than they would have in their own.

Isn't that the design of the family of God? Isn't that what God intended for His children? "And if one member suffers, all the members suffer with it; if one member is honored, all the members rejoice with it" (1 Cor. 12:26).

What the family of God urgently needs today are individuals who resonate with the heart of the Father, men and women who take great joy when others win. Their joy arrives when they accept the privilege of helping someone open their gifts and see their dreams take flight.

God extends to you His likeness. He extends to you His invitation. Dare we trust Him for His promises?

Nudge a dream into flight.

A whole generation awaits you.

TAKING ACTION

*I*dentify a few young potential leaders and formulate a plan to tap their cages and nudge them into flight. Dedicate the next season of your life to seeing their gifts begin to blossom. Begin by using the following suggested "curriculum":

- Identify those whom God may put on your heart.
- Pray for them daily.
- Invite them to do devotions with you at least once a week.
- Include them in activities, so they can observe how you live.
- Find a time to ask them about their dreams and what they think they can be for God.
- Help them to identify the greatest dream killers they face.
- Ask for permission to speak into their lives, should you detect a drift from God's direction.
- Applaud them with words of encouragement and inspiration.

Remember, this is exactly what Jesus did with the Twelve. And those who began as rough fishermen turned into those who changed the world.

ENDNOTES

Chapter One

1. Martin Luther King, Jr., "I Have a Dream," *Web66,* July 2002. http://web66.coled.umn.edu/new/MLK/MLK.html (accessed July 31, 2002).

Chapter Three

1. From HAPPY BIRTHDAY TO YOU! by Dr. Seuss, TM & copyright © by Dr. Seuss Enterprises, L.P. 1959, renewed 1987. Used by permission of Random House Children's Books, a division of Random House, Inc.

2. I am indebted to Dr. Myles Munroe for his message "Realizing Your Potential," given in 1995. His insights and perspective influenced me greatly in the writing of both chapters 3 and 4.

Chapter Seven

1. Alain Boublil, Herbert Kretzmer and Jean-Marc Natel (lyrics); Claude-Michel Schonberg (music), "I Dreamed a Dream," *Les Misérables* (New York: Alain Boublil Music Ltd, 1986).

2. Coolidge, Calvin, *The New Encyclopedia of Christian Quotations,* comp. Mark Water (Grand Rapids, MI: Baker Books, 2000), p. 726.

ABOUT THE AUTHOR

Dr. Wayne Cordeiro is senior pastor of New Hope Christian Fellowship in Honolulu, Hawaii; one of the nation's fastest growing churches. New Hope, on the island of O'ahu, is Wayne's eleventh pioneer work, opening it's doors in 1995.

Prior to relocating to O'ahu, Wayne pastored in Hilo, Hawaii for 12 years. He is a church planter at heart and has helped to plant 80 churches in the Pacific Rim and beyond, including Hawaii, Seattle, Los Angeles, Las Vegas, the Philippines, Japan and Myanmar. Today, New Hope continues to build and train leaders and pastors through the Pacific Rim Bible College founded by Wayne in 1998.

Wayne enjoys relaxing rides on his Harley-Davidson and is an author and songwriter. He is a contributing author for church leadership books and magazines and has authored seven books:

- *Doing Church as a Team*
- *Gems Along the Way*
- *Attitudes That Attract Success*
- *Rising Above*
- *Seven Rules of Success*
- *Culture Shift*
- *The Divine Mentor*

Wayne and his wife, Anna, have three children, Amy, Aaron and Abigail.

For more information about resources by Wayne Cordeiro, please write or call:

Life Essentials
290 Sand Island Access Road
Honolulu, HI 96819
Phone (808) 842-4242, ext. 604
www.Lifejournal.cc

You're also welcome to visit these websites:

www.eNHI.org
New Hope International Ministries

MentoringLeaders.org
Bringing world class mentors right to your desktop

www.prbc-hawaii.edu
Pacific Rim Bible College